Crypto Insight

Understanding Digital Assets

Joseph M. Maas

CFA, CFP®, CLU®, ChFC®, MSFS,
CCIM™, CVA, CM&AA, ABAR

Merrell Marketing, LLC
Vancouver, WA

Merrell

Neither the author nor the publisher is engaged in rendering financial, legal, or accounting services to the reader through the sale of this book. Since individual situations do vary, the reader should consult a competent professional on questions specific to the individual. The author and publisher disclaim any liability for loss incurred, directly or indirectly, as a consequence of the use or application of any information contained in this book.

Printed in the United States of America.

Merrell Marketing, LLC, Vancouver, WA
www.synergy-am.com
Library of Congress Cataloging-in-Publications Data

Crypto Insight: Understanding Digital Assets
/ Joe Maas – 1st ed.

Joseph M. Maas
Founder, Synergy Asset Management, LLC
13215 SE Mill Plain Blvd #C8-321
Vancouver, WA 98684
Phone: 206-386-5455 www.synergy-am.com

Disclaimer

This book is presented solely for educational purposes and is not intended to represent or be used as an exhaustive financial industry resource. The information contained in this book is made available for illustrative purposes, explaining only the basics of blockchains and cryptocurrencies.

The author, contributing author, and Merrell Marketing, LLC, emphasize this material is not offered as financial, legal, accounting, or other professional services' advice. It is highly recommended you seek the services of competent professionals before making any decisions regarding your business or personal finances.

Best efforts have underscored the writing of this book, but the author and publisher make no representations or warranties of any kind and assume no liabilities of any kind with respect to the accuracy or completeness of the contents, and specifically disclaim any implied warranties of use for any particular purpose.

Neither the authors nor Merrell Marketing, LLC, shall be held liable or responsible to any person or entity with respect to any loss or incidental or consequential damages caused, or alleged to have been caused, directly or indirectly, by the information contained in this book, or disruption caused by errors or omissions, whether such errors or omissions result from negligence, accident, or any other cause.

The reader is advised to consult with professional advisers with experience in cryptocurrencies and blockchains.

This book was originally written in 2018 and revised in 2025. While this book provides an excellent overview of cryptocurrencies and blockchains, the cryptocurrency industry is subject to rapid changes and the reader is cautioned to confirm all details.

In Memoriam

Zachariah "Zach" Paul Doty
1989 - 2023

Devoted family man, entrepreneur, advocate for liberty and passionate about mathematics, our friend was an early enthusiast of cryptocurrency and a contributor to this book. You are always in our hearts.

Dedication

This book is dedicated to my Lord and Savior, Jesus Christ, my loving wife, Molly, my precious princess, Madison, my amazing son, Andrew, my Church, my mother, Anne Maas, and in loving memory of my father, Henry Maas.

Acknowledgments

We wish to personally thank the following people for their help with creating this book:

Eryka Gemma for her many contributions to the expanded content of this book. Thank you for being a contributing author!

Frank Roman for his knowledge and contribution to the content of several chapters.

Our editor, Dr. Daniel Levine, for his patience, expertise, fine eye for detail, and considerable and necessary sense of good humor.

Lindsay Lush for consistently providing eye-catching and engaging book covers ... with a creative flourish!

Olivia Hobson; you continue to impress, and we appreciate the technical expertise you exemplify with every book project.

Mary Kate Robinson; you are not just the duct tape and steel that holds everything together; you are our joyful companion!

The Synergy staff for your contributions to this work, insightful advice, and consistently helpful reflections.

Synergy's valued clients; you inspire us to keep growing as professionals, and we delight in serving you.

Synergy Asset Management's RIAs and IARs ... You have made the Dream come true for all of us, and we are grateful. Thank you!

The Insight Series from Merrell Marketing

Available Now:

Exit Insight: Getting to "Sold!"

401(k) Insight: Getting to "Retired!"

Real Estate Insight: Creating Wealth Through Real Estate Investing

Advisor Empowerment: Getting to Independent

Money Insight: The Art and Science of Managing Money

Investment Insight: To Allocate or Concentrate

Crypto Insight: Understanding Digital Assets

Annuity Insight: Building Diversified Portfolios

Wealth Insight: Building Your Wealth Vision

New Book Coming Soon!

Marketing and Sales Insight: Getting to Conversions

Table of Contents

Preface

As a fiduciary investment advisor, the primary responsibility is to act in the best interest of clients and make informed investment recommendations based on thorough analysis and evidence. When it comes to the cryptocurrency ecosystem, several factors make it challenging to recommend these assets as a sound investment option.

First, the lack of sufficient fundamental evidence poses a significant hurdle. Cryptocurrencies operate in a relatively young and rapidly evolving industry. While they have gained attention and popularity, there is limited historical data and fundamental information available to conduct comprehensive analysis. This absence of traditional financial metrics, such as earnings, cash flows, or balance sheets, makes it difficult to assess the intrinsic value and long-term viability of cryptocurrencies.

Additionally, the overall maturity of the cryptocurrency industry itself is a concern. Regulatory frameworks are still being developed and then revised, and there is ongoing uncertainty surrounding legal and compliance aspects. The lack of standardized practices, transparency, and investor protections further contribute to the risk and uncertainty associated with cryptocurrencies.

Furthermore, investing directly in cryptocurrencies is often seen as speculative rather than a prudent investment strategy. The price volatility and rapid fluctuations in the cryptocurrency market make it challenging to predict future performance or determine appropriate valuation metrics. The speculative nature of cryptocurrencies increases the potential for significant losses, which can be detrimental to clients' financial well-being.

However, that does not mean there are no investment opportunities in the cryptocurrency ecosystem. Investing in the technologies surrounding the industry, such as blockchain technology or companies involved in developing cryptocurrency-related solutions, may offer a more grounded approach. These investments can be evaluated using traditional fundamental analysis, providing a more reliable basis for decision-making. Companies involved in providing infrastructure, security, or ancillary services to the cryptocurrency ecosystem might also offer more tangible and understandable investment options.

Drawing a parallel to the gold rush era, when companies selling picks, shovels, and mining supplies profited more than individual gold miners, a similar niche may apply in the cryptocurrency realm. Investing in companies that support the infrastructure or facilitate transactions within the industry can potentially offer more stable and diversified exposure without directly assuming the risks associated with individual cryptocurrencies.

In summary, as a fiduciary investment advisor, the current limitations and uncertainties surrounding cryptocurrencies make it difficult to recommend them as a sound investment option. The lack of fundamental evidence, industry maturity, and speculative nature pose challenges to the fiduciary duty of preserving and growing clients' wealth. Investing in companies involved in the technologies supporting cryptocurrency activity may offer a more grounded and potentially less risky approach, aligning with the fiduciary responsibility of making informed and prudent investment recommendations.

On the Flip Side: The Case for Including Digital Assets in a Diversified Portfolio

While the concerns surrounding cryptocurrencies — such as regulatory uncertainty, volatility, and the lack of traditional financial metrics — are valid, there is also a compelling argument for considering digital assets as a component of a well-diversified portfolio. The evolving regulatory landscape, increasing institutional adoption, and Bitcoin's improving performance characteristics suggest that a prudent allocation to cryptocurrencies, even if modest, may be beneficial.

One of the strongest arguments for incorporating digital assets is the increasing regulatory clarity and institutional adoption. Over the past several years, regulators have made significant strides in defining how cryptocurrencies are classified and governed. The approval of Bitcoin futures ETFs, the establishment of clearer compliance frameworks for digital asset custodians, and the growing acceptance of blockchain-based financial products indicate that cryptocurrencies are moving toward legitimacy in the financial ecosystem. As regulatory uncertainty diminishes, financial advisors may be in a better position to evaluate these assets through a more traditional risk-management lens.

Furthermore, Bitcoin, often referred to as "digital gold," has demonstrated unique characteristics as an asset class. While it remains volatile, its performance in risk-on environments suggests it is increasingly behaving like a cyclical asset rather than a purely speculative instrument. Bitcoin's four-year halving cycle and its growing correlation with macroeconomic trends, such as inflation expectations and liquidity cycles, make it more predictable than in its earlier years. Additionally, Bitcoin's scarcity (a fixed supply of 21 million coins) and decentralized nature have led some analysts to consider it a hedge against fiat currency depreciation, similar to gold.

From a portfolio construction perspective, small allocations to cryptocurrencies have demonstrated non-correlated or low-correlated return patterns compared to traditional equities and fixed income. Several studies have suggested that even a 1-3% allocation to Bitcoin in a diversified portfolio could enhance risk-adjusted returns by improving diversification benefits. As cryptocurrencies continue to integrate into the broader financial system, they may offer a potential upside while mitigating the risks of over-concentration in traditional asset classes.

In light of these considerations, financial advisors may need to re-evaluate the outright exclusion of cryptocurrencies from client portfolios. As the asset class matures and regulatory oversight improves, fiduciaries who fail to consider digital assets could be overlooking an emerging investment opportunity. A prudent approach would be to maintain a disciplined allocation strategy, incorporate rigorous due diligence, and educate clients on both the potential benefits and risks of digital asset exposure.

Ultimately, as the investment landscape evolves, so too must the methodologies and frameworks used by fiduciaries. While cryptocurrencies may not yet be a cornerstone of portfolio construction, their increasing relevance suggests they deserve thoughtful consideration rather than outright dismissal.

Special Note: As an RIA, you may find value with sending the following letter to your clients, with appropriate modifications, who inquire about investing in cryptocurrencies:

Dear Client,

I understand you may be interested in investing in cryptocurrencies and have raised concerns about why your financial advisor may not be recommending it as part of your investment portfolio. I want to provide you with an explanation that reflects the perspective of a financial advisor.

As a fiduciary financial advisor, our primary responsibility is to act in your best interest and make recommendations based on a thorough analysis of available information and the pursuit of long-term financial goals. When it comes to cryptocurrencies, there are several reasons why your financial advisor may be cautious or hesitant to recommend them:

Lack of Regulatory Clarity: The regulatory landscape surrounding cryptocurrencies is still evolving, and there is a lack of standardized practices and investor protections. This regulatory uncertainty introduces risks for investors, making it challenging to ensure compliance with legal and regulatory requirements.

1. Volatility and Speculative Nature: Cryptocurrencies are known for their high price volatility and rapid fluctuations. These price swings can be significant and occur within short periods, making it difficult to predict and assess the long-term performance or value of cryptocurrencies. The speculative nature of cryptocurrencies introduces a higher level of risk, which may not align with your risk tolerance or long-term financial goals.
2. Limited Fundamental Evidence: Traditional investment analysis relies on fundamental evidence, such as earnings, cash flows, and balance sheets, to assess the intrinsic value of an investment.

Cryptocurrencies, being a relatively young and evolving industry, lack comprehensive historical data and established fundamental metrics. This absence makes it challenging to perform a thorough analysis and make well-informed investment decisions.

3. Client Suitability and Risk Management: Your financial advisor takes into consideration your unique financial situation, goals, and risk tolerance when making investment recommendations. Cryptocurrencies may not align with your specific financial objectives or risk tolerance. Your financial advisor's recommendation is based on a comprehensive understanding of your needs and a desire to protect your financial well-being.

However, it's essential to note that your financial advisor may still recognize the potential value and growth of cryptocurrencies. They may be actively monitoring developments in the cryptocurrency market and evaluating opportunities as they arise. Your advisor's primary concern is to ensure that any investment recommendations are aligned with your financial objectives and are based on a thorough understanding of the risks involved.

If you are still interested in cryptocurrencies, your financial advisor may suggest alternative ways to gain exposure to the industry, such as investing in companies involved in blockchain technology or cryptocurrency-related solutions. These options may provide a more diversified and potentially less risky approach while still allowing you to participate in the potential growth of the cryptocurrency industry.

Ultimately, your financial advisor's primary goal is to guide you toward a well-diversified portfolio that aligns with your financial objectives and risk tolerance while minimizing unnecessary risks. They are committed to your long-term financial success and will continue to provide guidance and recommendations based on thorough analysis and prudent investment strategies.

If you have any further questions or would like to discuss this matter in more detail, I encourage you to reach out to your financial advisor. They are here to address your concerns and provide personalized guidance that takes into account your unique financial circumstances.

Sincerely, [Financial Advisor's Name]

Introduction

In today's rapidly evolving digital landscape, the emergence of cryptocurrencies and blockchain technology has transformed the way we think about money, investments, and financial transactions. The rise of digital assets has brought about new opportunities and challenges for individuals seeking to navigate this exciting frontier. In this book, *Crypto Insight: Understanding Digital Assets*, we cautiously explore the world of cryptocurrencies, blockchain, decentralized technology and the various aspects of managing digital wealth.

As the world of finance continues to evolve, it is imperative for financial advisors and their clients to stay ahead of the curve and embrace emerging opportunities. Cryptocurrencies, with their transformative potential and growing prominence, have become an integral part of this ever-changing asset class. This book has been meticulously crafted to bridge the knowledge gap and provide essential guidance to financial advisors and their clients as they consider the realm of cryptocurrencies and their integration into investment portfolios.

Understanding the intricacies of cryptocurrencies and their role in portfolio management can be daunting for even the most experienced financial professionals. Recognizing this need, we have dedicated our expertise to present a comprehensive resource to demystify cryptocurrencies, explore their potential benefits, and address the risks associated with their incorporation into investment portfolios.

Our primary objective is to equip financial advisors with the necessary tools and knowledge to educate and guide their clients in making informed decisions about cryptocurrencies. We recognize that, as trusted advisors, you have a responsibility to provide unbiased insights and expert guidance tailored to each client's unique financial goals, risk tolerance, and investment preferences. By offering clear explanations, practical examples, and actionable advice, we empower financial advisors to confidently navigate the complexities of the cryptocurrency landscape.

Simultaneously, we recognize the importance of engaging clients and enabling them to participate actively in their financial journey. This book serves as a valuable resource for clients seeking to better understand the potential of cryptocurrencies and their integration into their investment portfolios. We aim to provide accessible explanations, dispel myths, and offer practical strategies to help clients make informed decisions about incorporating cryptocurrencies into their broader financial plans.

Crypto Insight covers a wide range of essential topics, including the nature of cryptocurrencies, blockchain technology, historical context, investment strategies, risk management, and regulatory considerations. Each chapter is designed to build upon the previous one, providing a comprehensive framework that promotes understanding, confidence, and ultimately, better decision-making.

We recognize that the digital asset landscape is ever-evolving, and our goal is to equip financial advisors and clients with a solid foundation of knowledge that can adapt to future developments. We encourage ongoing engagement, continued learning, and staying abreast of regulatory changes and industry trends to ensure that the integration of cryptocurrencies into investment portfolios remains informed, strategic, and aligned with each client's unique financial objectives.

Together, let's enter the world of cryptocurrencies, embracing innovation and the potential they hold. We wish to help you become more familiar with this exciting new landscape with increased confidence, informed decision-making, and a commitment to achieving your financial goals.

As we get started, it's important to note that quite often, the words bitcoin, blockchain and crypto are used synonymously. This is incorrect and can be very confusing, and it is important to impress upon the reader the differences of these terms so the reader can appreciate and benefit from a more clear and distinct understanding.

Another important distinction is the capitalized and uncapitalized versions of Bitcoin/bitcoin. When capitalized, Bitcoin refers to the concept or network of Bitcoin; when lower case, bitcoin refers to a unit of account. Please note that this distinction is sometimes haphazard in the cryptocurrency ecosystem, so use your own best judgment when reading materials about this astonishing concept ... network ... and unit of account!

Chapter Overview

Chapter 1: What is Money? We begin our exploration by considering the fundamental concept of money. Understanding the nature and functions of money provides a solid foundation for comprehending the role of cryptocurrencies as a form of digital currency and alternative means of exchange.

Chapter 2: Blockchain Technology. Next, we look into the revolutionary technology that underpins cryptocurrencies: blockchain. We demystify the workings of blockchain, its ability to operate in a decentralized nature, and its potential to revolutionize industries beyond finance, such as supply chain management and data security.

Chapter 3: History of Bitcoin. To appreciate the context and origins of cryptocurrencies, we delve into the history of Bitcoin, the first and most well-known cryptocurrency. We explore the genesis of Bitcoin, its creator(s), and its subsequent impact on the financial landscape.

Chapter 4: Bitcoin Mining. Mining plays a vital role in the creation and maintenance of cryptocurrencies. We dive into the world of Bitcoin mining, examining the mining process, its significance, and the environmental and technological implications it entails. Also discussed are private keys, public addresses, and the significance of cryptography in safeguarding digital wealth.

Chapter 5: The Evolving Financial System. This chapter explores the new possibilities emerging as the blockchain paradigm is creating a parallel financial ecosystem based on public ledgers, not on the private financial systems of banks and governments.

Chapter 6: Ethereum. Bitcoin and other prominent cryptocurrencies have emerged, each with unique features and potential uses. We review the impact of the second biggest cryptocurrency, Ethereum, and its similarities and differences with Bitcoin.

Chapter 7: Emerging Cryptocurrencies, AKA Altcoins, and Wallets. The cryptocurrency ecosystem is constantly evolving, with new digital currencies, known as 'altcoins,' entering the scene. We explore the landscape of emerging cryptocurrencies, their innovative features, and the potential they hold for investors and technology enthusiasts.

Chapter 8: Government Involvement. Government and regulatory bodies play a crucial role in shaping the cryptocurrency landscape. We examine the involvement of governments, explore regulatory frameworks, and discuss the impact of government actions on cryptocurrencies taking into account the recent changes in national leadership.

Chapter 9: Investing in Digital Currencies. Investing in digital currencies carries unique considerations and risks. We provide insights into the strategies, platforms and best practices for investing so readers can make informed decisions about allocating their resources in this dynamic market.

Chapter 10: Bitcoin ETFs, Digital Assets on the Balance Sheet. In January 2024, U.S. regulators gave approval for exchange traded funds of bitcoin, marking the first time BTC (bitcoin) was available for trading at day-to-day prices. This exciting opportunity has changed the cryptocurrency ecosystem, further legitimizing BTC as an asset. This chapter describes the basics of the current situation with BTC ETFs.

Chapter 11: Crypto Asset Insights for Advisors and Their Clients. The CFA Research & Policy Center published a guide in November 2023 to inform registered investment advisors (RIAs) and other professional and interested parties about how to assess the validity and value of crypto assets, starting a discussion that will mature as the financial industry examines and potentially increases its acceptance of this new type of financial asset.

Chapter 12: Liquid Real Estate. Lastly, we study the concept of liquid real estate, examining innovative models and technologies that allow investors to tap into the liquidity of real estate assets using blockchain and tokenization.

Chapter 13: The Future of Blockchain and Crypto. The future of blockchain and cryptocurrencies is a subject of great interest and speculation. We consider the potential applications of blockchain beyond cryptocurrencies and delve into the possibilities and challenges that lie ahead.

In *Crypto Insight: Understanding Digital Assets*, we wish to provide readers with comprehensive insights about the world now made possible by blockchain technology, and explore the regulatory environment that is slowly but steadily adapting to this new form of digital currency and new asset category.

Though digital currencies are new, they are not complicated. When you approach this topic with an open and curious mind, you will come out the other side with some great ideas of your own.

Our hope is that this book provides you with the information you need to guide your clients toward effective participation in the digital revolution, and that it provides a new method for achieving financial security and independence.

Chapter 1

What Is Money?

The conceptual nature of money has expanded once again as the Digital Revolution continues to change all aspects of our society, from paper bills and metal coins to tapped plastic credit cards ... now we witness the birth of corporate efinancial systems accepting cryptocurrencies from ewallets. This chapter explains the value cryptocurrencies represent to the 21st century, exploring how cryptocurrencies are shaping the possibilities of our digital lives.

Objectives

In this chapter you will:

- Gain a deeper awareness of the purpose, functions, and forms of money.
- Possess a basic understanding of the purpose and functions of cryptocurrencies.
- Become more informed about the benefits and detriments of cryptocurrency as an investment asset class and its value as a form of currency.
- Be able to compare and contrast fiat money with cryptocurrency.
- Perceive the trends that have developed in the

cryptocurrency sector and consider how cryptocurrency may be used in the future.

- Learn the nine steps of incorporating cryptocurrency into your investment portfolio, should you choose to do so.
- Consider the value of establishing an Investment Policy Statement (IPS) for the cryptocurrency you may someday have in your investment portfolio.

Understanding Money: Its Nature and Function

Money is an essential part of our daily lives, serving as a medium of exchange, a unit of account, and a store of value. It plays a pivotal role in facilitating economic transactions and promoting economic growth. In this chapter, we will delve into the concept of money, its functions, and how it is used in modern societies.

The Nature of Money

Money can be defined as a universally accepted medium of exchange that is used to facilitate transactions and represent value. It takes various forms throughout history, including physical objects such as shells, metals, and paper, as well as digital forms in the modern era. Regardless of its physical or digital nature, money serves as a representation of economic value.

It is important to note that what is used as money is different from the payment channels that money is transferred upon, as differentiating between the two is important for the discussion of digital assets.

The Functions of Money

a. Medium of Exchange: The primary function of money is to serve as a medium of exchange, eliminating the need for barter. Money acts as a commonly accepted intermediary, enabling individuals to trade goods and services efficiently. By providing liquidity, it enhances the ease and convenience of transactions.

b. Unit of Account: Money acts as a unit of account, providing a standard measure for valuing goods, services, assets, and liabilities. It enables individuals to compare and determine the relative worth of different items in the market. Prices are denoted in monetary terms, allowing for easy comparison and evaluation.

c. Store of Value: Money serves as a store of value, allowing individuals to save purchasing power for future use. Unlike perishable or highly specific goods, money can be held and preserved over time without significant loss of value. People can accumulate wealth in the form of money, providing financial security and flexibility.

Traits of Money	Gold	Fiat (US Dollar)	Crypto (Bitcoin)
Fungible *(Interchangeable)*	High	High	High
Non-Consumable	High	High	High
Portability	Moderate	High	High
Durable	High	Moderate	High
Highly Divisible	Moderate	Moderate	High
Secure *(Cannot be counterfeited)*	Moderate	Moderate	High
Easily Transactable	Low	High	High
Scarce *(Predictable Supply)*	Moderate	Low	High
Sovereign *(Government Issued)*	Low	High	Low
Decentralized	Low	Low	High
Smart *(Programmable)*	Low	Low	High

Figure 1: The Traits of Money.

The Forms of Money

a. Physical Currency: Physical currency, such as coins and banknotes, has been used for centuries as a tangible representation of money. It offers a tangible and portable means of conducting transactions, although its usage has been declining in some areas with the rise of digital payment systems.

b. Digital Money: With the advent of technology, digital money has gained significant prominence. Electronic transactions through debit cards, credit cards, mobile payment apps, and online banking have become increasingly common. Digital money offers convenience, security, and instantaneous transferability.

Definition:
Money is a universally accepted medium of exchange that is used to facilitate transactions and represent value.

How Money is Used

a. Exchange of Goods and Services: Money is primarily used to facilitate the exchange of goods and services. It provides a common medium for individuals to acquire the necessities and desires of life. Money enables specialization and division of labor, driving economic growth and productivity.

b. Investment and Savings: Money allows individuals to invest in various assets, such as stocks, bonds, real estate, and businesses. Investment opportunities enable the growth of capital and potential returns, thereby fostering economic development. Additionally, money can be saved and accumulated for future needs or emergencies.

c. Economic Indicators: Money plays a crucial role in measuring and tracking economic activity. It serves as an essential component in various economic indicators, such as gross domestic product (GDP), inflation rates, and monetary aggregates. These indicators help policymakers and economists make informed decisions about economic policies and interventions.

Money is an indispensable part of modern society, serving as a vital tool for economic transactions, value representation, and financial stability. Its functions as a medium of exchange, unit of account, and store of value provide the foundation for economic interactions. As the world progresses, the forms and methods of money usage continue to evolve, adapting to technological advancements. Understanding the nature and utilization of money is crucial for individuals, businesses, and policymakers alike, ensuring efficient economic systems and sustainable growth.

Cryptocurrency: Serving the Triple Role of Money, Asset Class, and Payment Network

Bitcoin, blockchain and cryptocurrency are often used synonymously. This is inaccurate and can be very confusing for people trying to understand this new world of finance. Let's add some clarity to this issue!

Bitcoin is an invention created out of the need for a better form of money that does not fall under "central control". In the cryptocurrency ecosystem, central control refers to the presence of a single authority or entity that governs, manages, or oversees the operation, transactions, and decisions of a monetary network, as opposed to decentralized systems where control is distributed among participants.

This need was addressed by cryptographers from all over the world via open-source technology. If you are not familiar with open-source, it is software code that is publicly posted on the Internet, allowing anyone to be able to copy, paste, find bugs and submit updates to the source code.

Many open-source projects do not have a formal team behind them and are the brain child of online developer communities. Some of the most widely used technologies in the world are open source because of the ability and benefit of tapping into the knowledge of the global collective of developers who are using, and can improve, the software.

Bitcoin's open-source nature was a breakthrough for early cryptographers. They read the source code, understood its incredible potential and named the revolutionary technology behind Bitcoin with the term "blockchain". Blockchain has many use cases and is a horizontal innovation that will most deeply impact industries dependent on record keeping. Banking, supply chain management, energy management, real estate and healthcare are low hanging fruit likely to adopt this technology.

Blockchain's most notable feature is its ability to create a distributed ledger. Its most well-known use case is to create cryptocurrencies, and its most revolutionary feature is the creation of "smart contracts". A smart contract is a self-executing program stored on a blockchain that automatically enforces, verifies, or executes the terms of an agreement when predefined conditions are met. It eliminates the need for intermediaries, ensuring transparency, security, and efficiency in transactions.

Software developers around the world took the source code of Bitcoin, copied, pasted it and changed lines of code to develop their own use case of the blockchain technology. This led to "crypto currencies" becoming a widespread phenomenon where anyone with a little bit of technical knowledge can spin up a new cryptocurrency. At the end of 2023 there were approximately 25,000 cryptocurrencies worldwide, and about 40 of them had a market cap of over $1 billion. Not all cryptocurrencies are decentralized or even distributed, many are failed projects, and some were created just for fun.

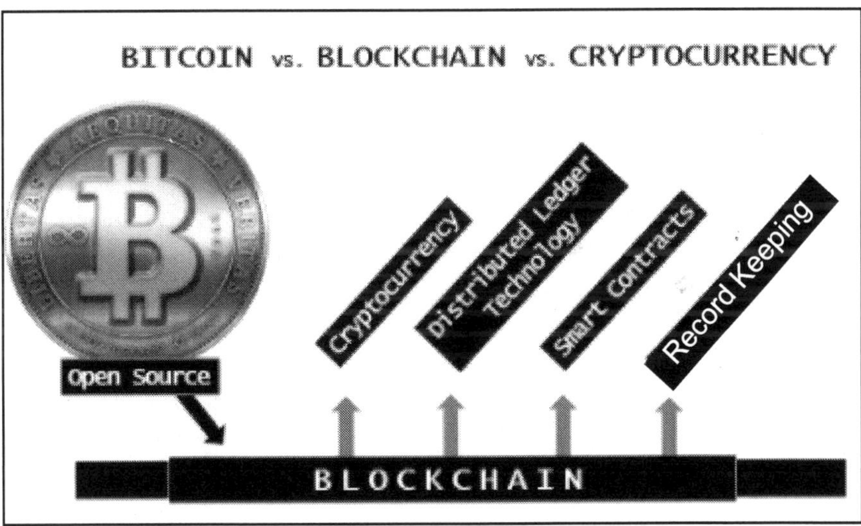

Figure 2: Blockchain Applications.

This graphic illustrates blockchain applications related to Bitcoin. Bitcoin is an open source invention that created the blockchain. All cryptocurrencies use a blockchain, but not all blockchain projects are cryptocurrencies; very few cryptocurrencies have the same economic features of Bitcoin.

Bitcoin, a digital form of currency based on cryptographic technology, has emerged as a revolutionary financial innovation. While cryptocurrencies were initially conceptualized as an alternative form of money, they have also evolved into a distinct asset class. In this chapter, we will explore the use of cryptocurrency both as a medium of exchange, as a payment network, and also as an asset class, highlighting the opportunities and challenges associated with each role.

Note:
Bitcoin has three distinct roles: A medium of exchange, a network platform, and an asset class.

Bitcoin as Money

a. Decentralization and Security: One of the key advantages of Bitcoin is its decentralized nature. This decentralization ensures transparency, and resistance to fraud or manipulation. As a result, cryptocurrencies provide individuals with direct control over their funds, enabling peer-to-peer transactions without intermediaries.

b. Efficient Cross-Border Transactions: Cryptocurrencies are revolutionizing cross-border transactions, eliminating the need for traditional intermediaries and reducing transaction costs and processing times. They can facilitate faster, cheaper, and more accessible remittances and international payments, particularly in regions with limited banking infrastructure. This removal of capital controls has created several billions of dollars of volume in the world of remittances alone.

Key:
Bitcoin's development as open-source technology produced blockchain technology, and cryptocurrencies became the first widely known use case. Cryptocurrencies are a new form of digital money based on a decentralized ledger called a blockchain.

c. Financial Inclusion: Cryptocurrencies hold the promise of enhancing financial inclusion by providing access to financial services for the unbanked and underbanked populations. With just a smartphone and Internet connection, unbanked individuals can now participate in the global economy, overcoming barriers associated with traditional banking systems.

d. Volatility and Adoption Challenges: The use of Bitcoin as a medium of exchange faces challenges due to its inherent price volatility and the nascent nature of the industry's rapid price fluctuations, making it challenging to determine the value of goods and services in bitcoin. However the creation of stablecoins have solved the volatility issue entirely. Additionally, limited merchant acceptance and regulatory uncertainties hinder widespread adoption for everyday transactions.

Cryptocurrency as an Asset Class

a. Potential for Investment Returns: Bitcoin has gained popularity as an alternative investment asset class. Investors are attracted to their potential for high returns, often driven by speculative trading and market dynamics. Bitcoin has demonstrated significant value appreciation over time, leading to wealth accumulation for early adopters. Bitcoin has evolved so far that it is now on the balance sheet of publicly traded companies and set records in the ETF world.

b. Diversification and Portfolio Allocation: Cryptocurrencies offer diversification benefits to investment portfolios. Their relatively low correlation with traditional asset classes, such as stocks and bonds, provides opportunities for risk mitigation and potential higher risk-adjusted returns. As a result, institutional and retail investors have increasingly considered cryptocurrencies as part of their investment strategies. Bitcoin is seen as a hedge against inflation as its economic characteristics are not inflationary.

c. Risk and Volatility: The cryptocurrency market is characterized by high volatility and inherent risks. The lack of regulatory oversight, market manipulation, cybersecurity threats, and technological vulnerabilities make investing in cryptocurrencies highly speculative. Prices can experience substantial fluctuations, leading to potential losses for investors. Bitcoin's volatility is often one of the biggest concerns for investors, however it should be noted that Bitcoin is historically more volatile to the upside.

d. Regulatory Environment and Institutional Adoption: The regulatory landscape surrounding cryptocurrencies is evolving, with authorities seeking to establish frameworks to address investor protection, market integrity, and financial stability concerns. Increased regulatory clarity can attract institutional investors, leading to enhanced liquidity, market stability, and broader adoption.

The 2024 election was a major win for the digital asset industry as a strong majority of pro-crypto candidates won their race. The House and Senate both gained an overwhelming majority of pro-crypto members.

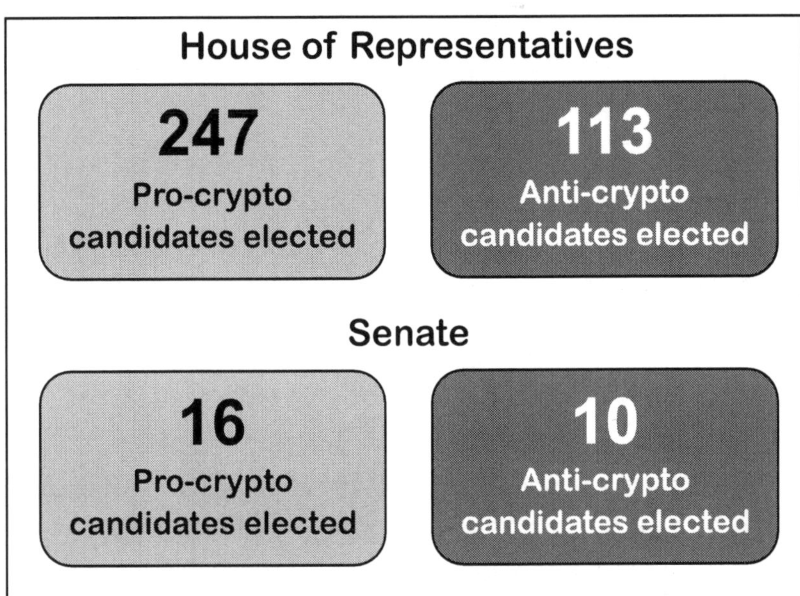

Figure 3. US Congressional Election Results, November 2024.

Cryptocurrencies have emerged as a multifaceted phenomenon, serving as a potential form of money, a payment network, and a distinct asset class. While their efficiency and potential for financial inclusion make them an attractive medium of exchange, challenges related to volatility and adoption hinder their widespread use as money.

Simultaneously, as an investment asset class, cryptocurrencies offer potential returns and diversification benefits, but their risks and regulatory uncertainties should be carefully considered. The future of cryptocurrencies will depend on striking a balance between their utility as money and their role as an investment vehicle while also addressing their associated challenges to create a more sustainable and inclusive financial ecosystem.

Comparing and Contrasting Traditional Money and Bitcoin

Traditional money, represented by fiat currencies issued by governments, and cryptocurrencies, such as bitcoin, are distinct forms of currency with unique characteristics. Let's compare and contrast the two in several key aspects:

Centralization vs. Decentralization

Traditional Money: Fiat currencies are centralized, meaning they are issued and regulated by central banks or governments. This central authority controls the supply, circulation, and monetary policies, influencing factors like interest rates and inflation.

Bitcoin: Bitcoin is relatively decentralized, operating on a distributed ledger called blockchain. It is not controlled by any central authority, relying on consensus mechanisms, game theory, computing power and cryptography for security and transaction validation. The control over cryptocurrencies lies in the hands of the network participants.

Legal Status and Regulation

Traditional Money: Fiat currencies have legal tender status, meaning they are recognized and accepted as a form of payment within a specific jurisdiction. Governments regulate traditional money, imposing monetary policies, consumer protections, and anti-money laundering measures.

Cryptocurrencies: The legal status of cryptocurrencies varies across jurisdictions. While some countries have embraced and regulated cryptocurrencies, others have imposed restrictions or bans. The regulatory landscape is evolving, with authorities addressing concerns like investor protection, taxation, and market integrity. There has also been discussion about Bitcoin's legal status, and concerns about self-custody wallets.

Stability and Value

Traditional Money: Fiat currencies, backed by the trust and confidence in the issuing government or central bank, aim for stability. Governments control the supply and can employ monetary policies to manage inflation and stabilize their currencies' value. However, fiat currencies can experience fluctuations due to economic factors and geopolitical events.

Note:
As cryptocurrencies grow in popularity, they may be more frequently used for purchases.

Cryptocurrencies: Cryptocurrencies are known for their price volatility, often experiencing significant fluctuations in short periods. Their value is primarily determined by market demand and sentiment. While this volatility can lead to substantial gains, it also poses risks for investors and challenges their use as stable mediums of exchange.

Accessibility and Inclusivity

Traditional Money: Traditional money is widely accessible as it is generally accepted and used by the majority of individuals and businesses. It is backed by established financial infrastructure, including banks, payment processors, and regulatory frameworks. However, accessibility can be limited in areas with inadequate banking services or unstable economies.

Key:

The IRS classifies cryptocurrencies as a property or digital asset, which means the owner will pay capital gains taxes if the cryptocurrency is exchanged with a profit.

Cryptocurrencies: Cryptocurrencies offer financial inclusivity by providing access to financial services for the unbanked and underbanked populations. They operate globally, independent of traditional banking systems, and require only a smartphone and an Internet connection. However, widespread adoption is hindered by limited merchant acceptance and technical barriers for non-tech-savvy individuals.

Privacy and Security

Traditional Money: Traditional money transactions often involve intermediaries like banks, which keep records of financial activities. While privacy can be protected within legal limits, transactions can be traced and monitored by authorities. Security measures, such as encryption and fraud detection, are implemented by financial institutions.

Bitcoin: Transactions on blockchain networks are transparent and traceable, although pseudonymity is maintained. Many networks prioritize security through cryptographic protocols, but some networks have cybersecurity risks.

Traditional money and bitcoin differ significantly in their centralization, legal status, stability, accessibility, and privacy features. Traditional money benefits from established infrastructure, stability, and regulatory frameworks, while Bitcoin offers decentralization, inclusivity, and potential financial innovation.

Both have their advantages and challenges, and their coexistence in the financial landscape offer individuals and businesses options for financial transactions and investments. As technology advances and regulations evolve, finding a balance between the two will be crucial for encouraging financial innovation while ensuring consumer protection and market stability.

The Future

The future of cryptocurrencies is a subject of much speculation and debate. While it is challenging to predict with certainty, several trends and possibilities can be considered:

1. Increased Mainstream Adoption: Cryptocurrencies are gradually gaining acceptance and recognition from mainstream institutions. Major companies such as Tesla, PayPal, and Square accept cryptocurrencies as payment. Additionally, some countries are exploring the idea of central bank digital currencies (CBDCs), which could further legitimize and integrate bitcoin or other cryptocurrencies into existing financial systems.

2. Regulatory Frameworks: The regulatory landscape for cryptocurrencies is evolving. Governments worldwide are actively working on establishing regulatory frameworks to address concerns such as investor protection, market integrity, taxation, and money laundering. Clear and well-defined regulations could enhance market stability and investor confidence, encouraging wider adoption.

3. Institutional Investment: Institutional investors, including hedge funds, asset managers, and banks are

increasingly considering cryptocurrencies as investment assets. The entry of institutional players brings liquidity, professional expertise, and credibility to the market. The launch of regulated cryptocurrency investment products such as exchange-traded funds (ETFs) could attract more institutional investors. In 2024, nearly half of all traditional hedge funds worldwide included cryptocurrencies in their investment strategies.

4. Integration of Blockchain Technology: Cryptocurrencies are built on blockchain technology, which offers benefits beyond currency transactions. This decentralized ledger has the potential to revolutionize various sectors, including supply chain management, healthcare, finance, and voting systems. As blockchain technology is maturing, it is finding wider adoption and driving innovation in banking and finance technology. Certain notable acquisitions have occurred by the DTCC in order to upgrade the settlement system for the stock exchanges.

5. Interoperability and Scalability Solutions: The current cryptocurrency ecosystem faces challenges related to scalability, transaction speed, and interoperability between different blockchain networks. However, ongoing research and development efforts aim to address these issues through solutions like layer-2 protocols, cross-chain interoperability, and scaling solutions. Overcoming these challenges could enhance the usability and efficiency of cryptocurrencies.

6. Environmental Concerns and Sustainability: The environmental impact of cryptocurrencies, particularly the energy consumption associated with bitcoin mining, has come under scrutiny. As sustainability

concerns grow, there will likely be a greater emphasis on developing more energy-efficient consensus mechanisms and transitioning to greener alternatives, such as proof-of-stake (PoS) consensus algorithms.

Over the years, the criticisms of energy consumption have shown as a net positive for the energy grid. It has been said that "Satoshi's second gift" is green energy because Bitcoin incentivizes green energy innovation. If you look at the clean energy landscape, there isn't much incentive to innovate other than tax breaks or feeling good about your choices.

Bitcoin miners are highly incentivized to lower their costs due to the "halving" effect of bitcoin. Their largest cost has always been energy, and now, because of the miners, the waste-gas run-offs from oil refineries that were polluting the environment can be captured to support the new global financial system, cutting emissions and providing a once-unusable form of energy.

This is just one example of the new clean energy solutions that have come about because of the emphasis bitcoin mining has placed on finding less expensive and more efficient sources of power. Publicly traded companies like CleanSpark, initially a green energy company, has changed their entire strategy to become a facilitator of bitcoin mining.

Another notable benefit to the energy sector brought about by Bitcoin is related to the power grid. In Texas, one of the most favorable states toward bitcoin mining, the power grid loves its bitcoin miners. Why? The grid has the ability to rapidly power up and power down the miners' use of energy as needed. The power grid is healthier when the use of power is constant.

For example, on a hot Texas day, consumers will run their AC higher at the peak heat hours – this power fluctuation is not ideal for the longevity of the grid. When bitcoin miners utilize the same grid, the power company can call miners and ask them to pull back their usage during peak hours so the grid can maintain a constant power flow. When the consumers turn their AC off, miners are given the green light to ramp up again.

7. Technological Innovation: The cryptocurrency space is dynamic and driven by technological innovation. New cryptocurrencies, blockchain platforms, smart contracts, and decentralized applications (dApps) continue to emerge, offering novel features, scalability improvements, and enhanced user experiences. Technological advancements, such as advancements in privacy and security features, may shape the future direction of cryptocurrencies.

It is important to note that the future of cryptocurrencies is not without risks and challenges. Volatility, regulatory uncertainty, security vulnerabilities, and potential market manipulation remain concerns that need to be addressed. The successful future of cryptocurrencies will depend on striking a balance between innovation, regulation, and widespread adoption, ensuring long-term stability, security, and utility.

How Do I Put Cryptocurrencies in My Portfolio?

Incorporating cryptocurrencies into your investment portfolio requires careful consideration and a balanced approach. Here are some steps to help you navigate the process:

1. Educate Yourself: Before investing in cryptocurrencies, it is essential to gain a solid understanding of how they work, their underlying technology, and the associated risks. Familiarize yourself with different cryptocurrencies, their use cases, and the market dynamics surrounding them. Stay updated with news, research reports, and expert opinions to make informed investment decisions. We now have access to new products and services for efficient, global record keeping.

2. Define Your Investment Goals and Risk Tolerance: Clearly define your investment objectives and assess your risk tolerance. Cryptocurrencies can be highly volatile and speculative, so determine the portion of your portfolio you are willing to allocate to this asset class based on your risk tolerance and financial goals. See the Investment Policy Statement (IPS) below.

3. Diversify Your Portfolio: Diversification is crucial for managing risk in any investment portfolio. Consider diversifying across different asset classes, including stocks, bonds, and real estate, in addition to cryptocurrencies. Diversification helps mitigate the impact of volatility and reduces exposure to any single asset.

4. Choose a Reliable Exchange or Brokerage: Select a reputable cryptocurrency exchange or brokerage platform that aligns with your investment needs. Research their security measures, user experience, trading fees, available cryptocurrencies, and regulatory compliance. Ensure the platform provides reliable and secure custody for your digital assets.

5. Conduct Due Diligence on Cryptocurrencies: Before investing in a specific cryptocurrency, conduct thorough research. Evaluate factors such as the team behind the project, the technology, adoption potential, market liquidity, and the overall market sentiment. Review the whitepaper, community engagement, and recent developments to assess the viability and potential risks.

6. Determine Investment Strategy: Decide on your investment strategy based on your risk tolerance and investment horizon. You can consider strategies such as long-term holding, dollar-cost averaging (regularly investing a fixed amount over time), or active trading based on technical or fundamental analysis. Each strategy has its own benefits and risks, so choose one that aligns with your goals.

7. Secure Your Crypto Assets: Cryptocurrency security is crucial due to the prevalence of hacking and scams in the digital asset space. Use secure digital wallets to store your cryptocurrencies and enable additional security measures such as two-factor authentication (2FA). Consider hardware wallets for offline storage, important due to their irreversible nature, providing an added layer of protection against cyber threats.

8. Monitor and Rebalance: Regularly monitor your cryptocurrency investments and the overall performance of your portfolio. Due to the volatility of cryptocurrencies, their weightings in your portfolio may change over time. Rebalance your portfolio periodically to maintain your desired asset allocation and risk profile.

9. Stay Informed and Evolve: The cryptocurrency market is dynamic and rapidly evolving. Stay updated with industry trends, regulatory changes, and technological

advancements. Continually assess your investment strategy and make adjustments as necessary to adapt to the changing landscape.

Remember, investing in cryptocurrencies involves risk, and past performance is not indicative of future results. Seek professional advice if needed and only invest funds you can afford to lose.

The Investment Policy Statement (IPS)

An investment policy statement (IPS) outlines the objectives, constraints, and guidelines for an investment portfolio. While the specific objectives and constraints can vary based on individual circumstances, here are two common objectives and five common constraints typically included in an IPS, along with their relevance to investing in cryptocurrencies:

Objectives:

1. Capital Appreciation (Return): The primary objective for many investors is to achieve capital appreciation, seeking long-term growth in the value of their investment portfolio. This objective aligns with investing in cryptocurrencies as they have the potential for significant price appreciation over time. However, it's important to note that cryptocurrencies are highly volatile and speculative, and their inclusion in the portfolio should be based on risk tolerance and long-term investment horizon.

2. Diversification (Mitigating Risk): Diversification is an objective aimed at spreading investment risk across different asset classes. It helps mitigate the impact of volatility and potential losses associated with any single

investment. Including cryptocurrencies in the portfolio can contribute to diversification as they have historically exhibited low correlation with traditional asset classes such as stocks and bonds. However, the degree of diversification achieved will depend on the allocation percentage and the specific cryptocurrencies chosen.

Constraints:

1. Risk Tolerance: Risk tolerance is a crucial constraint that determines the acceptable level of risk an investor is willing to assume. Investing in cryptocurrencies can be highly risky due to their price volatility and regulatory uncertainties. An IPS should consider the investor's risk tolerance and set appropriate limits on the allocation to cryptocurrencies, ensuring it aligns with the investor's comfort level.

2. Liquidity: Liquidity constraint refers to the ease with which an investment can be bought or sold without significantly impacting its price. Cryptocurrencies are generally highly liquid, with 24/7 trading availability. However, during times of extreme market volatility, liquidity can become limited, leading to challenges in executing trades at desired prices. Investors should consider the liquidity constraints of cryptocurrencies when determining their allocation in the portfolio.

   Liquidity in a portfolio can also refer to the availability of funds. It serves as a buffer to meet immediate or short-term financial needs, such as daily expenses, emergency funds, or planned expenses within the next year. Maintaining an appropriate level of liquidity ensures that the portfolio can fulfill these spending requirements without having to sell long-term investments prematurely or incurring unnecessary fees.

3. Time Horizon: The time horizon is the length of time an investor intends to hold the investments in their portfolio. Cryptocurrencies can be suitable for long-term investments as they have the potential for significant growth over extended periods. However, due to their volatility, short-term investments in cryptocurrencies may carry higher risk and are not typically recommended for investors with a shorter time horizon.

4. Regulatory and Legal Considerations: Cryptocurrencies operate in a regulatory environment that is still evolving. The regulatory and legal considerations constraint in an IPS should take into account any legal restrictions or regulations concerning the purchase, holding, or sale of cryptocurrencies in the investor's jurisdiction. Compliance with applicable laws and regulations is essential to ensure the investment aligns with legal requirements.

5. Investment Policy Guidelines: Investment policy guidelines establish specific rules and restrictions for the investment portfolio. They may include limits on the maximum allocation to cryptocurrencies, rebalancing thresholds, and risk management strategies. These guidelines should be designed to align with the investor's objectives, constraints, and risk tolerance and provide a framework for making informed decisions regarding cryptocurrencies within the portfolio.

Definition:

An investment policy statement outlines the objectives, constraints, and guidelines for an investment portfolio.

In summary, an IPS for investing in cryptocurrencies should consider objectives such as capital appreciation and diversification, while also addressing constraints such as risk tolerance, liquidity, time horizon, regulatory considerations, and specific investment policy guidelines. It should be tailored to the investor's individual circumstances and risk preferences to guide the prudent inclusion of cryptocurrencies in the investment portfolio.

Chapter 1: Review Questions

1. Which of the following is correct? Money is:

   A. A unit of account.

   B. A store of value.

   C. A medium of exchange.

   D. A and C only.

   E. A, B and C.

2. True or false? Money can take any tangible or intangible form of exchange providing people accept it as having value.

   A. True.

   B. False.

3. Which of the following is true? Money can be used:

   A. For the exchange of goods and services.

   B. For investment and savings.

   C. As an economic measurement.

   D. All of the above.

4. Cryptocurrency is a fiat form of currency based on cryptographic technology. True or false?

   A. True.

   B. False.

5. Which of the following statements are true?

   A. Cryptocurrency is a distinct asset class.

   B. Cryptocurrency is an indispensable part of modern society.

C. Cryptocurrency is a form of money.

D. Only A and C.

E. Only A, B and C.

6. Cryptocurrencies are creating problems with cross-border transactions. True or false?

A. True.

B. False.

7. Which of the following are false? As an asset class, cryptocurrencies:

A. Have a potential for investment returns.

B. Can be used to diversify portfolio allocations.

C. Are characterized by high volatility.

D. Do not yet have regulatory clarity or uniformity worldwide.

E. Only A and B.

F. Only A and C.

G. All of the above.

8. True or false? Cryptocurrencies are centralized, and traditional money is decentralized.

A. True.

B. False.

9. An Investment Policy Statement (IPS) is helpful because it:

A. Outlines your investment objectives.

B. Identifies your investment constraints.

C. Acts as a guideline for your investment portfolio.

D. Focuses only on short-term investments.

E. Details how much of your paycheck should be invested every month.

F. All of the above.

10. True or false? Cryptocurrencies are gradually gaining recognition and acceptance as a form of payment.

A. True.

B. False.

Chapter 1: Review Answers

1. Which of the following is correct? Money is:

A. A unit of account.

B. A store of value.

C. A medium of exchange.

D. A and C only.

E. A, B, and C.

Answer: E. A, B, and C are correct. Money serves all three of these functions: a unit of account, a store of value, and a medium of exchange.

2. True or false? Money can take any tangible or intangible form of exchange providing people accept it as having value.

A. True.

B. False.

Answer: A. True. Money can take any form, as long as people are willing to accept the form as a unit of exchange.

3. Which of the following is true? Money can be used:

A. For the exchange of goods and services.

B. For investment and savings.

C. As an economic measurement.

D. All of the above.

Answer: D. All of the above. Money is an indispensable part of modern society, serving as a vital tool for economic transactions, value representation, and financial stability.

4. Cryptocurrency is a fiat form of currency based on cryptographic technology. True or false?

A. True.

B. False.

Answer: B. False. Cryptocurrency is a digital form of currency based on cryptographic technology, not a fiat form guaranteed as legal tender by a government.

5. Which of the following statements are true?

A. Cryptocurrency is a distinct asset class.

B. Cryptocurrency is an indispensable part of modern society.

C. Cryptocurrency is a form of money.

D. Only A and C.

E. Only A, B and C.

Answer: D. Cryptocurrency is being adopted as an additional form of currency by many nations around the globe, and it is also a distinct asset class people can invest in.

6. Cryptocurrencies are creating problems with cross-border transactions. True or false?

A. True.

B. False.

Answer: B. False. Cryptocurrencies have the potential to revolutionize cross-border transactions. They can facilitate faster, cheaper, and more accessible remittances and international payments, particularly in regions with limited banking infrastructure.

7. Which of the following are false? As an asset class, cryptocurrencies:

A. Have a potential for investment returns.

B. Can be used to diversify portfolio allocations.

C. Are characterized by high volatility.

D. Do not yet have regulatory clarity or uniformity worldwide.

E. Only A and B.

F. Only A and C.

G. All of the above.

Answer: E, F, and G are false. They are the only false answers as A, B, C and D are correct.

8. True or false? Cryptocurrencies are centralized, and traditional money is decentralized.

A. True.

B. False.

Answer: B. False. Traditional money is centralized, meaning it is controlled by a central government, while cryptocurrencies are decentralized, meaning no single person or group has control.

9. An Investment Policy Statement (IPS) is helpful because it:

A. Outlines your investment objectives.

B. Identifies your investment constraints.

C. Acts as a guideline for your investment portfolio.

D. Focuses only on short-term investments.

E. Details how much of your paycheck should be invested every month.

F. All of the above.

Answer: A, B, and C. An IPS helps you by identifying your objectives and your limitations, and serves as a guide for your current investments and investments you would like to acquire in the future.

10. True or false? Cryptocurrencies are gradually gaining recognition and acceptance as a form of payment.

A. True.

B. False.

Answer: A. True. Tesla, PayPal, and Square are a few of the major companies who now accept cryptocurrencies as payment.

Chapter 2

Blockchain

Blockchain technology may be new to you, but remarkably it has been available for over a decade. Don't feel embarrassed if you don't know much about it, as it is only now becoming more popularly acknowledged in our culture's consciousness. Originally discovered due to the open source advent of Bitcoin, many people are now becoming aware of the multitude of applications this new system offers. The ability to secure data without the control of third-party organizations like banks is just the tip of the iceberg. Because of the expected influence of blockchain technology in your life, here are the important details you'll need to know!

Objectives

In this chapter you will:

- Know what a blockchain is and does.
- Gain insight to why blockchains may become a life-changing phenomenon.
- Read about some examples of how blockchains currently being developed are coming into use today.
- Learn why blockchains are secure from fraudulent activity.

- Understand what a hash is and why it's important.
- Become familiar with the value of a distributed ledger.
- Realize the importance of proof of work.
- Perceive the value of the time stamp algorithm created by Haber and Stornetta.
- Learn what the "double spend" problem is and how it was solved.
- Comprehend the increasing pervasiveness of digital currency in our lives today.
- Understand how blockchain technology supports the existence of cryptocurrencies like bitcoin and Ethereum.

What Is Blockchain?

Blockchain is a fairly new application of technology which many of today's leading thinkers strongly believe is the next world-changing phenomenon. Just as the personal computer dramatically changed our lives, which in turn was augmented by the Internet extending our ability to communicate and connect with each other in unforeseen ways, so now it is anticipated that blockchain technology will also make an emphatic and thorough conversion to the way we live.

Personal computers and the Internet have allowed us to communicate more completely with each other through the exchange of emails, text, and videos in the realms of business, our social lives, and for personal interest through the acquisition of data. In its own unique way this aspect of technology has helped us expand our knowledge of the world, rapidly increase our interactions with each other, and improve our lives in a variety of ways depending on the enthusiasm we expend in the pursuit of our personal interests.

Now comes blockchain technology ... the next step at the intersection of the human experience with computer technology. In its essence, blockchain is simply a continuously updated record of data that secures proven information by consensus, removing the need for validation by third-party intermediaries.

Why is this significant? Why not just continue with the way things are? Everything is working just fine as it is, right? Not so fast! We live in a world where change is a constant, and blockchain technology is a revolutionary invention that can apparently improve our quality of life, save time, save money, and make normal interactions more convenient and expedient.

The truth of the matter is that no one really knows exactly how blockchain technology will change the way we live because it is still too soon to tell. Remember and imagine it's the mid-1990s and desktop computers with Microsoft software are starting to populate business offices and homes. Email and online shopping are fairly new to most people. Making hotel reservations or buying your groceries online, comparing automobile prices or arranging travel routes by Google Maps were an unthought-of fantasy. Could everyone foresee the advent of Facebook or Amazon? No, of course not. It took a few visionaries experimenting with ideas about how to use this then-new technology to eventually pull the entire world along to where we are today.

Today's visionaries and captains of industry are telling us that blockchain technology is still in its Tin-Lizzie days, pioneering now what will someday lead to the metaphoric bedazzling of unimagined superhighways or super-jet travel. Once again technology is providing new opportunities for experimentation and potential success for those who are bright enough, quick enough, and lucky enough to establish a new empire based on the myriad possibilities blockchain technology offers. Someday years from now we may all say, "Ah-ha! Why didn't I think of that?" because whatever it is that then exists will seem so obvious and so normal.

So, now that you have the beginning of an idea about what blockchain technology is and the barest indication of what it does ... let's take a look at what makes the blockchain such an attractive data repository.

Definition:

Blockchain: A continuously updated record of data that secures proven information by consensus, removing the need for validation by third-party intermediaries.

First of all, the word blockchain represents what its name indicates, which is a chain of blocks. Each block contains information; the information could be about anything that is important enough to maintain accuracy. For example, the information could be about real estate ownership, or about the pedigree of a show dog, or about medical or dental records. Of course, it could also be about a form of electronic currency like a Bitcoin. Whatever data is in the block, it is important enough to want to maintain its accuracy.

Note:
A block contains information that is important to keep accurate.

Each block of data in the chain contains three elements:

1. The data

2. The hash of the block

3. The hash of the previous block

The word “hash” refers to the unique set of sequenced numbers and letters that identify only this one block. (See Figure 5 and Figure 6 in Chapter 4.) The hash is like a fingerprint because it is unique and can never be changed. If any of the data in the block is changed, then the hash changes also. There can only be one hash for each block of data.

Important:
A hash is like a fingerprint; it is unique to only one block.

A blockchain, aside from being a chain of blocks with data and unique hash identifiers, is also a distributed transparent ledger that can be seen by anyone. What does this mean? The blockchain is a ledger because it contains data. It’s transparent because anyone who wants to look at the contents of any block can do so; there are no restrictions on observing the contents of a block. The blockchain is considered to be distributed because a copy of the blockchain is sent to everyone wanting to be part of a particular blockchain network.

For example, if you're a professional breeder of golden retrievers, it's probably important to keep track of the sires, the bitches, the breeders, the size of the litter, and other data that secures important information about American Kennel Club (AKC) pedigreed golden retrievers. While there may not yet be a blockchain for dog breeds, it's reasonable to expect that someday one will be created to help secure information about the lineage of the breed.

Important:
A distributed ledger is available to everyone in the blockchain network.

Because of the importance of this information, there will probably be many breeders who will want to join the pedigree golden retriever blockchain. Each block in the chain will contain data about the breed, or about specific dogs, about the sires, about champion show dogs, etc., forming a ledger that anyone will be able to study. This blockchain will be distributed to all the members of the blockchain group so each breeder or each interested party will be able to see the contents of the blockchain.

Everyone will have access to the same information, and it will not be controlled by a third-party organization like the AKC. The AKC could be a member of the blockchain and have access to the contents of the blockchain, but they will no longer control the data. The data will belong to the blockchain network who now has responsibility for maintaining the accuracy of the blockchain. As mentioned, each block has its own unique hash, or unique set and sequence of number and letter identifiers. When a block is created it's hash is calculated and set. Changing anything inside the block will make the hash change to a new hash. Everyone in the blockchain network will know that the content of the block has changed because the hash is different. This helps maintain the integrity of the chain because if something in the block is changed, everyone will know, and are quite likely to investigate. Also as mentioned, each block contains the hash of the previous block, making the sequence of legitimate blocks secure and extremely difficult to be tampered with successfully. The links that connect the chain of blocks make a blockchain secure.

For example, imagine a blockchain with 10 blocks. The first block in a blockchain is called the genesis block. If someone tampers with the second block, the hashtag of the second block will change, making the third block and all the subsequent blocks invalid because the second block was changed incorrectly. Each block in the chain is like a brick in a strong brick wall, one brick built upon the other. If someone tampers with a brick, the whole wall is damaged and everyone in the blockchain group knows it. Even so, hashes by themselves are not enough to prevent tampering. Computers can be relentless, and a determined person could use the efficiency and speed of computers to make changes to the hash and all the hashes that follow, so another safety, or integrity, protocol exists called "proof of work".

Important:
Proof of work consumes computer resources to solve a complex algorithm, which contributes to the security of the block and the blockchain.

When a person in the blockchain group creates a new block, they are required to generate proof of work. At this point it is easy to get into the weeds about how the proof of work is established, so suffice it to say that an algorithm is created that typically requires computational difficulty, and when resolved, the result is regarded as the proof of work. The proof of work is then verified by members of the blockchain network and accepted if it is valid.

Because the proof of work is time-consuming and requires efficient computation and high electrical usage, tampering with the proof of work for all the blocks that follow a block that has been compromised, and thus recalculating the paperwork for every one of the subsequent blocks creates an exponential amount of work, and is regarded as a waste of time and resources not worth the effort. A massive amount of servers and electrical energy would be needed, which becomes unprofitable.

But even so, there is yet another hurdle to overcome in the case of a person committed to fraudulent behavior, and that is the protocol of consensus. As mentioned before, every member of the network has their own copy of the blockchain because a blockchain is a distributed ledger. A blockchain is a peer-to-peer network that anyone can join. When a person joins the network, they are regarded as a "node", a fancy name for a member.

Definition:
Node: A member of a blockchain network.

When a new block is created, all the nodes on the network receive it and each node verifies the validity of the new block. When a minimum of 51% of the nodes confirm the validity of the new block, the new block is added to the chain. Because validity is achieved with no less than 51% of the network confirming, a person intent on benefiting from fraud would have to control at least 51% of the network, which is currently regarded as impossible to do.

Therefore, if someone chose to tamper with the blockchain, they would have to adjust the hash for every block subsequent to the fraudulent block, and dedicate costly resources to generating a new proof of work for each of the tampered blocks, and also control at least 51% of the peer-to-peer network. Could it be done? The community believes this is impossible.

In a Nutshell

In its essence, blockchain is an open decentralized public database or ledger of any transaction that involves items of value. Items of value can be money, real estate, other forms of property such as goods, copyrighted or proprietary work, or data such as notarized paperwork, medical records, or the ancestry of pedigreed animals. The blockchain creates a record whose authenticity can be verified by the nodes of the community. This decentralized database is updated periodically and is stored on every node's computer.

Just as personal computers and the Internet have established a peer-to-peer community that has broadened, streamlined, and expedited our ability to communicate with each other and acquire data independent of controlling institutions, so now it is expected that blockchain technology will threaten the existence of third-party trust organizations such as banks or governments that until now have controlled the flow of data in their role as intermediary.

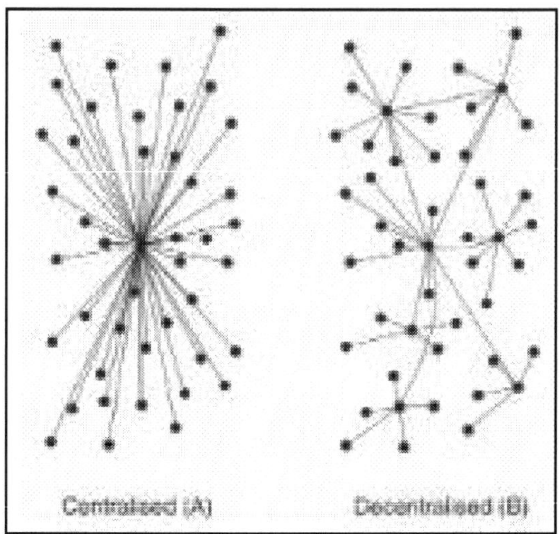

Figure 4: The Difference Between a Centralized Network and a Decentralized Network.

Now the information is secured through (a) the cryptography of hash, (b) detailed proof of work, and (c) the consensus of the network nodes.

The History of Blockchain Technology

Blockchain technology was first described in 1991 by a pair of computer researchers who were trying to find a way to time stamp digital documents in such a way that it would be impossible to back-date documents or tamper with them electronically. As you know, it's very easy to change a digital document. In a matter of moments you can change the content, font style, font size...everything.

So Stewart Haber and W. Scott Stornetta were trying to find a way to authenticate digital documents. In a sense, they were working on a way to develop a foolproof digital notary with an unaltered time stamp. The riddle they were trying to solve was, "How can we time stamp a document so no one can ever change the date electronically?"

Key:

The cryptography used by blocked chains employs a complicated mathematical formula that allows input and gives output, but does not allow reversing to solve for the inputs.

Their solution was to use cryptography by employing a complicated mathematical formula that takes input and gives output, but does not allow reversal. Here is a simplistic example: 2 + 3 = 5 ... but the formula Haber and Stornetta used would not permit starting with 5 and subtracting 3 to get 2.

Their cryptographic equation allowed input to get output, but prevented reversing the equation to solve for the inputs. This formula made the time stamp immutable. When applied to a blockchain, the time stamp could not be changed without clearly being recognized as fraudulent.

This was the first step in the security of blockchain technology development. This advance also solved what was known as the "double spend problem". The work of Haber and Stornetta went mostly unused for the next 18 years, until 2009 when someone realized an application for their cryptographic formula.

The Double Spend Problem

The double spend problem is specific to the authenticity of digital currency. It's the risk that a digital currency could be spent twice, or three times, or a million times. Double spending is a problem unique to digital currencies because digital representation can be easily copied and reproduced.

When you have a digital asset, what is preventing you from spending it twice? What will stop you from paying two people with the same digital dollar bill?

Note:
The double spend problem was resolved so digital currency could not be spent twice.

In the physical world, you can't give the same dollar bill to two different people at the same time because the physicality of the coin or paper prevents it from being used twice simultaneously. However, in the electronic world, you could copy digital currency and send the same unit to as many people as you wish. This is cheating of course, and is similar to a counterfeiter who physically prints the same dollar bill with the same serial number and spends the counterfeit money in different places. What prevents you from doing this with a digital currency?

The formula used by Haber and Stornetta, when applied to a currency blockchain, solves this problem because each block of the currency has a unique fingerprint, or hash, for each digital coin. The formula prevents people from artificially duplicating the coin and solves the double spend problem.

Cryptocurrency

Very simply, cryptocurrency is digital currency that serves two purposes. First, cryptocurrency uses cryptography to regulate the generation of additional units of currency. Second, cryptocurrency uses cryptography to track the transfer of value.

It's no surprise that most of us are using digital currency in our daily lives. When you go to the bank and deposit paper in the form of a check or paper money, your deposit is digitally registered and shows up on a computer screen when you look for it in your account. When you use your credit or debit card at the gas station or when buying supplies at the market, you are using a form of digital currency.

Note:
Digital currency already permeates our culture and business transactions.

You are transacting for goods and services with a digital currency that is controlled by a third-party like a bank or a credit union. The bank is taking responsibility for debiting and crediting the buyer and the seller, and in many cases the bank takes a thin slice of the transaction for itself or makes up for its service with fees or penalties if triggered. The bank is in business to make money and does not serve its customers or members strictly from the goodwill of its inherently benevolent nature. Ha!

There are presently several kinds of digital currencies as our society becomes increasingly cashless. Debit and credit cards are one form, bank wires are another, and funds held on computers for trading in the stock market or held in escrow by banks and lending institutions are all forms of digital currency. Cryptocurrency is a subset of digital currency.

Cryptocurrency is unique because of its two special attributes:

1. Cryptocurrency can be authenticated because it is protected by its hash, its documented proof of work, and

by the consensus of the nodes in its network.

2. Cryptocurrency is not controlled by a third-party because as a distributed database, its information is stored in every node's computer, preventing interference with the transactions. You might think of cryptocurrency as a democratic currency instead of an autocratic currency.

How Blockchain Is Used for Digital Currency

At this point you can now see how the pieces fit together. With the advent of computers and the Internet, an independent form for communicating with each other was established. Subsequently, a means was developed for protecting digital documentation. As with so many things in our contemporary culture, a digital environment has made inroads to our physical environment, leading most people to live with a well-planted foot in each world. Slowly but inexorably we are becoming a cashless society more and more as digital currency steadily replaces coins and bills.

Cryptocurrency, a form of digital currency, gained credence because it can be protected against fraud and, as will be revealed, cryptocurrency can be employed to save time and money. Blockchain technology provides the backbone for an immutable decentralized ledger which, for the first time in history, enables the transfer of value without a third party intermediary.

Blockchain technology is a decentralized system that allows transactions to be recorded without a central authority like a bank or financial institution. It accomplishes this by storing a copy of every block with every transaction that has ever occurred on all the network nodes.

Key:

"Many nations are now developing their own cryptocurrency. As of February 2023, 114 countries, including the United States, are considering introducing their own central bank digital currencies (CBDCs) to compete with the cryptocurrency boom."[1]

This means that instead of a single set of data controlled by a single entity storing everyone's transaction history, the data is stored instead on thousands of independent computers. The benefit is that if one computer or node fails, no data is lost because there are thousands of identical copies simultaneously stored on thousands of computers.

Summary

Blockchain technology is being used now for digital currency, but digital currency is only one of the many applications of the blockchain. Blockchains are currently being considered for land registry in Sweden and the Honduras, by the diamond industry to prevent the blood diamond trade, for insurance claims processing, for encrypting votes to prevent hacking and fraud, to protect the property rights of musicians, to protect and confirm health records, secure logins and passwords with SSL certificates stored on a blockchain, to record disease data that helps expedite disaster relief response, to create

[1] Council on Foreign Relations. *"Cryptocurrencies, Digital Dollars and the Future of Money"*, February 28, 2023.

a blockchain-based SKU supply chain, to focus on anti-counterfeiting in luxury goods, to keep track of legitimate pharmaceuticals...and the list continues.

These are just some of the applications for blockchains, with more being developed regularly. It's remarkable to realize that this new technology has become pervasive so quickly when it has only fairly recently been accepted as a viable system with global implications. Most of the world's major banks and industries are considering how to use blockchain technology, and very soon you are likely to see its presence become more visibly dominant in your personal and professional life.

Chapter 2: Review Questions

1. "Proof of work" refers to:

A. The amount of work each node does to stay in the network

B. An integrity protocol that adds security

C. A node's required amount of work to retain membership in the blockchain network

D. Proof that the block originated in the United States

2. The reason each block, except for the genesis block, contains the hash of the previous block is so that each block is in its proper sequence in the chain.

A. True

B. False

3. The main reason why blockchain technology is considered a world-changing phenomenon is because:

A. Blockchain technology prevents fraud

B. Blockchain technology can speed up the transmission of data

C. Blockchain technology can save money

D. Blockchain technology eliminates third-party control

E. Blockchain technology is transparent

F. A and B above

G. A, B and D above

H. All of the above

4. A distributed ledger is a collection of data distributed to selected nodes in a blockchain network.

A. True

B. False

5. The protocol of consensus means:

A. A 2/3 majority of the nodes in the network must approve the new block

B. 51% of the nodes in the network must approve the new block

C. The originator of the block must do 51% of the proof of work

D. All of the above

6. A block chain is a chain of blocks that contain information which must be kept accurate.

A. True

B. False

7. Blockchain technology secures information through:

A. All of the following

B. The consensus of the network nodes

C. Detailed proof of work

D. The cryptography of hash

8. The cryptography formula that Haber and Stornetta used was an equation that allowed input to arrive at output, but blocked reversing the equation to solve for the inputs.

A. True

B. False

9. When a hash is changed:

A. The network accepts the change as standard operating procedure

B. Every node records the change and changes the hash on the other blocks to match

C. Everyone in the block chain network knows the content of that block was also changed

D. The person changing the hash pays a 10% penalty

10. Blockchain technology has become available only in the last two years.

A. True

B. False

11. The double spend problem is:

A. A puzzle the nodes must solve to make a new block

B. A level of cryptography that creates a genesis block

C. Preventing digital currency from being replicated and spent twice

D. An algorithm that allows digital currency to be spent twice

12. Cryptocurrency is unique because it is not controlled by a third-party like a bank or other financial institution.

A. True

B. False

Chapter 2: Answers

1. "Proof of work" refers to:

A. The amount of work each node does to stay in the network

B. An integrity protocol that adds security

C. A node's required amount of work to retain membership in the blockchain network

D. Proof that the block originated in the United States

Answer: B. Proof of work is required every time a new block is added to the chain. Because the proof is complex and requires a great deal of computer calculation, this layer of security is one of several that together protect the blocks and the chain from being compromised.

2. The reason each block, except for the genesis block, contains the hash of the previous block is so that each block is in its proper sequence in the chain.

A. True

B. False

Answer: A. True. Because each block has the hash of the previous block imprinted on it, the network knows the data in the new block is the next unit of information in the chain.

3. The main reason why blockchain technology is considered a world-changing phenomenon is because:

A. Blockchain technology prevents fraud

B. Blockchain technology can speed up the transmission of data

C. Blockchain technology can save money

D. Blockchain technology eliminates third-party control

E. Blockchain technology is transparent

F. A and B above

G. A, B and D above

H. All of the above

Answer: H. All of the above. Blockchain technology can save time and money, is fraud-proof, eliminates the middleman, and anyone in the network can see the contents of the blocks.

4. A distributed ledger is a collection of data distributed to selected nodes in a blockchain network.

A. True

B. False

Answer: B. False. Every node in a blockchain network receives the contents of the chain.

5. The protocol of consensus means:

A. A 2/3 majority of the nodes in the network must approve the new block

B. 51% of the nodes in the network must approve the new block

C. The originator of the block must do 51% of the proof of work

D. All of the above

Answer: B. A minimum of 51% of the members, or nodes, in the blockchain network must agree that the new block is bonafide before the block can be added to the blockchain.

6. A block chain is a chain of blocks that contain information which must be kept accurate.

A. True

B. False

Answer: A. True. Each block in the chain contains data that is important to the network, and must be accurately recorded.

7. Blockchain technology secures information through:

A. All of the following

B. The consensus of the network nodes

C. Detailed proof of work

D. The cryptography of hash

Answer: A. All of these required protocols together provide protection against the admission of fraudulent blocks to the blockchain.

8. The cryptography formula that Haber and Stornetta used was an equation that allowed input to arrive at output, but blocked reversing the equation to solve for the inputs.

A. True

B. False

Answer: A. True. Because a person intent on fraudulent behavior cannot reverse the output to determine the inputs, a timestamp cannot be modified. This keeps the dating of the block accurate and secure.

9. When a hash is changed:

A. The network accepts the change as standard operating procedure

B. Every node records the change and changes the hash on the other blocks to match

C. Everyone in the block chain network knows the content of that block was also changed

D. The person changing the hash pays a 10% penalty

Answer: C. The purpose of the hash is to uniquely identify a specific block in the chain. If anyone tampers with the block, the hash changes and that alerts everyone in the network that the data in the block is different and suspect.

10. Blockchain technology has become available only in the last two years.

A. True

B. False

Answer: B. False. Blockchain technology has been available for over a decade.

11. The double spend problem is:

A. A puzzle the nodes must solve to make a new block

B. A level of cryptography that creates a genesis block

C. Preventing digital currency from being replicated and spent twice

D. An algorithm that allows digital currency to be spent twice

Answer: C. Because digital data can be

manipulated, researchers had to find a way to prevent digital currency from being duplicated and used improperly.

12. Cryptocurrency is unique because it is not controlled by a third-party like a bank or other financial institution.

A. True

B. False

Answer: A. True. Cryptocurrency is on a distributed database, not in a third-party database, making the exchange between buyer and seller more efficient, more timely, and less expensive than transacting through a third party.

Chapter 3

History of Bitcoin

As you know by now, Bitcoin has been around only a very short period of time, and yet has become wildly popular. Like most good ideas that are made material, the concept has led to an active system in which millions of people participate. Much like we saw the explosive applications of computers spread quickly throughout the workplace, into homes, and now are carried about in the palms of our hands in the form of smart phones and other variations of the technology, so also has Bitcoin permeated our business and social consciousness and advanced our concept and use of the interchangeability of modern currency in the 21st century.

Still in its infancy, much like the wheel was first applied to the oxcart, then to bicycles, and subsequently to the moon rover, the evolution of Bitcoin will be fascinating to watch. To observe the evolution means to know something of its origin. This chapter serves a twofold purpose: to provide a brief history of how Bitcoin got started; and provide some basic information about transaction fees.

Objectives

In this chapter you will:

- Be introduced to the work of several leading digital cryptographers who contributed to the development of blockchain and Bitcoin.
- Learn about a few digital currency predecessors of Bitcoin.
- Become as perplexed as everyone else about the mysterious identity of Satoshi Nakamoto.
- Understand the difference between Bitcoin and Bitcoin.
- Find out about the only flaw that ever threatened the feasibility of the blockchain and Bitcoin systems.
- Know more about how transaction fees are set and by whom.

The History of Bitcoin

Before Bitcoin was first released, there were already several digital cash technologies that existed. Possibly the first form of electronic money was developed from an idea presented in a research paper by David Chaum in 1983. If you can remember that far back, you'll remember that this was when the Digital Age was just beginning. Clunky computers, the big desktop models, were showing up in offices everywhere, and also on a few classroom tables in the back of the room. It's remarkable to realize that at the dawn of computer accessibility, someone was already thinking about a way to exchange currency digitally.

In 1990, David Chaum founded his company in Amsterdam and called it DigiCash. The company used eCash software and was protected cryptographically by a bank. Digital money could be sent to any shop that participated; in 1998 the company filed for bankruptcy.

Another company was E-gold, founded in 1996 and backed by gold, and yet another company was called Liberty Reserve, founded in 2006, allowing participants to convert either US dollars or euros into Liberty Reserve dollars or euros for exchange with participants, and it imposed a 1% transaction fee. Both services were centralized and did not use blockchain technology. Concerns about money laundering eventually led to the demise of both operations. Q coins or QQ coins were another form of ecurrency, popular in China.

A pioneer in cryptographic protocols was Dr. Stefan Brands. He worked with David Chaum to resolve the issues of security and privacy, and eventually his work proved sound and was accepted by a number of banks and European IT organizations. Another pioneer was Adam Back, the developer of hashcash, a proof-of-work system to protect information from manipulation and fraud. Hashcash was originally developed as a means for controlling spam.

Key:
Privacy and security were paramount issues for the early developers of cryptocurrency.

Underlying the development of cryptocurrency and the possible systems of information and value transmission between participants was the clear concern of these pioneers for the privacy and security, not just of currency and wealth, but the rights of individuals to protect information about themselves and avoid the promiscuity of invasive databases and the collection of information that might lead to the circumstances foreseen by George Orwell and the nightmare of Big Brother.

We are still struggling with these issues today...and perhaps blockchain technology, which can legitimately eliminate the prying eyes of governmental inquisitiveness and the criminal behavior of determined hackers, could be a solution. Witness the pandemonium caused by Facebook's privacy foibles, or the occasional hacking of personal information and credit card data from millions of every-day citizens as a sign of the need for improvement.

However, improving on the preceding ideas, in 1998 a person named Wei Dai proposed a cryptocurrency called "b-money", proposing an "anonymous, distributed electronic cash system", which sought to develop a system where anonymous people could exchange currency with each other for goods and services without being controlled or regulated by a third-party.

Also in 1998, a computer scientist and cryptographer named Nick Szabo designed a digital currency system called "bit gold". Bit gold remained academic only and was never implemented, but is regarded as the direct predecessor of Bitcoin. In his proposal, Szabo defined a system that required the dedication of computer power for solving a complex cryptographic puzzle that would secure the content being protected, would carry the public pseudonym of the cryptographer who solved the puzzle, and require approval from the majority of participants before moving on to the next puzzle.

This was the extent of cryptocurrency advances because of the obstacle of figuring out a solution to the double spend problem. The double spend problem, you'll recall, was finding a way to prevent digital currency from being copied, pasted and fraudulently reused.

It wasn't until 2004 that another computer scientist who was also a computer game developer named Hal Finney invented a system that could store and transfer proof of work validation in a chain system. This was a major step forward in protecting the security of information.

Important:

Finney lived in Temple City, California, a small city of about 35,000 people in the Northeast section of Los Angeles County.

Satoshi Nakamoto

A few more years went by and then, in 2008, Wei Dai and Adam Back were contacted by a person who called himself Satoshi Nakamoto. To this day, no one knows the identity of Satoshi Nakamoto. People love a mystery, especially cryptographers, but this mystery had limited solutions because in the first decade of the 21st century there weren't many techno-philosophers with the credentials to resolve the complex issues necessary to give birth to the reality of a bona fide and secure cryptocurrency system.

And yet, somehow an advanced computer scientist with visionary tendencies had flown under the radar all those years and surfaced with a solution for the even bigger mystery of how to create a secure cryptocurrency.

The identity of this person, or perhaps a group of computer experts masquerading as Satoshi Nakamoto, remains a mystery. Speculation has pointed to Wei Dai, and Nick Szabo, and Hal Finney, but all three have declined the honor and claim innocence. Here is the little we do know about Satoshi Nakamoto, the creator of Bitcoin.

The first known appearance of Satoshi Nakamoto was through the posting of a link to a whitepaper written by Satoshi Nakamoto appearing in a cryptography mailing list on October 31, 2008, which curiously was also Halloween. The paper was titled "Bitcoin: A Peer-to-Peer Electronic Cash System". This was the first anyone had heard of Bitcoin, but research later established that a domain name for Bitcoin.org was registered on August 18, 2008, about 10 weeks before the publication.

As you read the Abstract, not only will you see how much you already know about blockchains, but you will also note that Satoshi Nakamoto claimed to provide the last link of the chain, pun intended, for creating a workable electronic cash system by solving the double spend problem.

Here is the opening paragraph of the whitepaper, available in full on the Internet:

> "**Abstract.** A purely peer-to-peer version of electronic cash would allow online payments to be sent directly from one party to another without going through a financial institution. Digital signa tures provide part of the solution, but the main benefits are lost if a trusted third party is still required to prevent double-spending.
>
> We propose a solution to the double-spending problem using a peer-to-peer network. The network timestamps transactions by hashing them into an ongoing chain of hash-based proof-of-work, forming a record that cannot be changed without redoing the proof-of-work. The longest chain not only serves as proof of the sequence of events witnessed, but proof that it came from the largest pool of CPU power.

> As long as a majority of CPU power is controlled by nodes that are not cooperating to attack the network, they'll generate the longest chain and outpace attackers. The network itself requires minimal structure. Messages are broadcast on a best effort basis, and nodes can leave and rejoin the network at will, accepting the longest proof-of-work chain as proof of what happened while they were gone."[2]

By virtue of writing this whitepaper, Satoshi Nakamoto became the designer of the currency known as Bitcoin, and by implementing the protocol for Bitcoin, the first blockchain database was established. The development of Bitcoin continued until December 2010.

Because Satoshi Nakamoto remained so incorporeal, it's hard to know what influenced his, or her, or their thoughts in combining or rejecting concepts that eventually led to the solution for guaranteeing a secure cryptocurrency system that had been under deliberation for about 15 years.

In January 2009, about two months after the release of the whitepaper, the Bitcoin network became a reality with the issuance of the first Bitcoins and with Satoshi Nakamoto mining the first block, or genesis block, with its reward of 50 Bitcoins. In the first transaction ever, Hal Finney received 10 bit coins from Nakamoto. It's estimated that Nakamoto mined about 1 million Bitcoins before disappearing and "assigning" further guidance to developer Gavin Andresen who became the lead at the Bitcoin Foundation.

---

[2]"*Bitcoin: A Peer-to-Peer Electronic Cash System*", Satoshi Nakamoto. https://Bitcoin.org/Bitcoin.pdf

Eight months later, on August 6, 2010, a flaw was discovered in the Bitcoin protocol when transactions were not verified properly before being included in the blockchain. This let users skip past the restrictions and develop an unknown number of new bitcoins. On August 15, over 184 billion (yes, billion) bitcoins were created in a single transaction and distributed to two addresses on the network. Before long, however, the transaction was erased and the vulnerability was repaired. The network then forked into a new updated version with a tighter protocol, and since then there has been no other major security flaw in Bitcoin's history.

Note:

Satoshi Nakamoto's accounts show the ownership of approximately 1 million bitcoins, worth more than $19,000,000,000 U.S. in December 2017, making Nakamoto the 44th wealthiest person on the planet. These bitcoins remain unused and closely watched by the Bitcoin network. There is speculation that the founder of Bitcoin has died or lost his access key.

Because almost everyone likes a mystery, a curious fact to ponder is that there was actually a Japanese computer engineer named Dorian Satoshi Nakamoto living in Temple City, California, not far from Hal Finney's home, and he vehemently denied any relationship to the mysterious originator of Bitcoin...so whether Hal Finney, the computer game programmer with a penchant for pseudonyms, was the author of the whitepaper and used the name of his unsuspecting neighbor, or was a ghostwriter for the real or imagined Satoshi Nakamoto, or was Satoshi Nakamoto himself, or truly never had anything to do with Satoshi Nakamoto, we are likely to never know!

Note:

If Satoshi Nakamoto ever did spend some bitcoins, it could cause a massive ripple across the market because the founder would likely be using the bitcoins that remained untouched since their origination...possibly leading to the biggest reveal in cryptocurrency history.

Transaction Fees

Whenever a person with a bitcoin conducts a transaction on the Bitcoin network, they need to pay a transaction fee. Transaction fees are paid in bitcoins. The transaction fee pays for the processing of the transaction, and for having the transaction confirmed by the network.

The fee rate, known as feerate, varies depending on the size of the transaction and also on how quickly the person initiating a transaction wants the transaction to be completed. Some people are in more of a hurry than others and may be willing to pay a higher transaction fee to speed up the process.

The transaction fee, curiously, is set by the person initiating the transaction, not by the miner who would be processing the transaction. If a person initiating a transaction offers a small transaction fee, the request for processing may have to wait until a miner agrees to accept this lower and less attractive fee. Higher fees are more likely to generate interest and therefore their transaction is likely to be processed more rapidly than smaller fees.

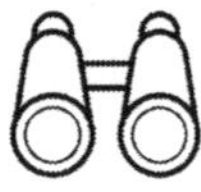

Definition:

Feerate: The fee offered by the initiator of a transaction to miners for processing and confirming the transaction.

In truth, miners don't make the decision to accept a transaction; they set their computers to hunt for transaction fees within a certain range, and select transactions that match the preset parameters. When the high fee transactions have been completed, the computers then look for other work with lesser fees. Typically, no transaction has to wait more than 24 hours to be processed. Depending on a person's urgency, a high transaction fee can be set for faster processing. A miner is paid the amount of the transaction fee when that block becomes a part of the blockchain.

Today there are thousands of transactions being made every minute, and statistically a new block is created on average every 10 minutes, though there are times when a block can be created within a few seconds or may take as long as an hour or more.

Summary

It's curious to reflect on the development and use of digital currency in our society, advancing from ink and paper ledgers in the 1980s to digital records held by third-party banks and financial institutions in the 1990s, to the 21st century transmission of encrypted digital currency between willing participants of an independent network who accept a new form of ethereal value with cryptocurrencies like Bitcoin and Ethereum.

Cryptocurrency technovisionaries have discovered applications and protocols that secure data, as well as monetary value, offering a new category of alternative investment opportunity for investors interested in expanding their portfolios to create wealth through a 21st century digital development and diminish their overall portfolio risk through allocation and diversification.

Chapter 3: Review Questions

1. The main reason for the delay in advancing digital cryptocurrencies was:

   A. The double spend problem

   B. The identity of Satoshi Nakamoto

   C. Transaction fees were too high

   D. Too much computer power was required

2. The Bitcoin protocol has only evidenced a single flaw in its reliability.

   A. True

   B. False

3. Who is Satoshi Nakamoto?

   A. Wei Dai

   B. Nick Szabo

   C. Adam Back

   D. David Chaum

   E. Hal Finney

   F. No one claims to know for sure

4. Bitcoin was the first-ever digital cash technology.

   A. True

   B. False

5. A major concern of early technophilosophers was:

A. None of the following

B. All of the following

C. The availability of the network to interested participants

D. The privacy of all participants

E. The security of the digital information

6. Statistically, a new block can be created in a few seconds, or take as long as 24 hours, but on average takes about 10 minutes.

A. True

B. False

Chapter 3: Answers

1. The main reason for the delay in advancing digital cryptocurrencies was:

    A. The double spend problem

    B. The identity of Satoshi Nakamoto

    C. Transaction fees were too high

    D. Too much computer power was required

    Answer: A. Early developers didn't know how to prevent a digital currency from being spent twice.

2. The Bitcoin protocol has only evidenced a single flaw in its reliability.

    A. True

    B. False

    Answer: A. True. Transactions were improperly verified, allowing users to circumvent restrictions and create billions of unauthorized Bitcoins. The flaw was discovered and eliminated, and the Bitcoin protocol has not been compromised since then.

3. Who is Satoshi Nakamoto?

    A. Wei Dai

    B. Nick Szabo

    C. Adam Back

    D. David Chaum

    E. Hal Finney

    F. No one claims to know for sure

Answer: F. The identity of Satoshi Nakamoto remains publicly unknown at present.

4. Bitcoin was the first-ever digital cash technology.

A. True

B. False

Answer: B. False. Preceding Bitcoin were several experimental digital currencies such as hashcash and b-money. However, Bitcoin was the first successful digital currency because it was protected from the double spend problem.

5. A major concern of early technophilosophers was:

A. None of the following

B. All of the following

C. The availability of the network to interested participants

D. The privacy of all participants

E. The security of the digital information

Answer: B. All of the following, as it was important that interested people have access, privacy, and secure exchanges.

6. Statistically, a new block can be created in a few seconds, or take as long as 24 hours, but on average takes about 10 minutes.

A. True

B. False

Answer: A. True. The speed of the transaction depends on the ability of the miners to solve the complex algorithm, which sometimes occurs instantly.

Chapter 4

Cryptocurrency Mining

Because no central authority can generate Bitcoins, such as the Federal Reserve does with printed paper money or by minting metal coins, Bitcoins must be created through an operation known as mining. In this chapter you'll learn how Bitcoins are mined, and have a more complete understanding of the complexity involved with creating cryptocurrencies.

Objectives

In this chapter you will:

- Understand how cryptocurrency is mined.
- Know the three most prominent proofs that secure the integrity of a block.
- Decide if mining for cryptocurrency is something you'd like to do.
- Be familiar with the terms users, nodes, and nonce.
- Realize why consensus is so important to a blockchain network.
- Learn how blocks are connected in a blockchain.
- Be able to explain what a hash is.

- Identify the two ways a miner is compensated.
- Have a better understanding about why scaling is a problem for blockchains.
- Develop an appreciation for the four benefits blockchains provide.
- Gain insight to the potential danger of a cabal controlling a blockchain network.
- Learn the difference between a private key and a public key.
- Know what a Wallet Import Format is and how it's used.
- Understand the purpose of a public address.
- Realize that Bitcoin may not be the best cryptocurrency for your investment, and why.

Cryptocurrency is generated when a new block is added to the blockchain. Before the new block can be added, however, a miner must find the one-and-only hash that belongs to that block. In order to solve the complex algorithmic problem that's based on specific requirements, miners compete against each other and calculate as fast as possible to be the first to identify the right hash, which is part of the process of showing the "proof of work".

Miners and Mining

To be a successful miner today, you need a computer and a special software program that allows your computer to mine. Years ago it was possible to compete with limited computing power, but today the algorithms are more complex and require so much technology that miners have to band together and combine their computing resources so they can compete against server farms making rapid calculations. Today, most miners have to spend much of their mining income just to pay for the large amount of electricity they are consuming!

Key:
Mining requires a vast amount of computing power to compete, with the Bitcoin network presently generating 5.5 quintillion hashes every second.

The first miner to create the hash that correctly solves the algorithmic problem is eligible to be rewarded. At today's rates, the miner with the correct hash receives 12.5 Bitcoins when the hash they calculated is accepted by the consensus of the network.

Users, Nodes, and Miners

There are three different levels of participation in the blockchain and they are called users, nodes, and miners.

- **User:** Most of the participants on a decentralized network are users who send and receive payments from other users and pay a small fee to the miners for verifying transactions. The normal, everyday person of cryptocurrency to buy goods, services, or to invest is called a user.
- **Nodes:** A node, also known as a full node, is a person using a program that validates transactions and blocks. Almost all full nodes also help the network by accepting transactions and blocks from other full

nodes, validating and relaying them to other full nodes to achieve consensus. To operate a full node, a person would need a broadband connection with speeds at a minimum of 50kbs and very high upload limits.

- **Miner:** A miner is a full node that adds to the blockchain by creating new blocks created from the new transactions relayed from other nodes. A miner verifies the transactions made by users and contributes to the process of consensus.

Transactions and Consensus

Consensus is the way cryptocurrency transactions are verified throughout the network, achieved by gaining at least a 51% approval of what has or hasn't happened. When a user sends a payment to another user, the payment from the user's eWallet is broadcast across the network automatically by the user's eWallet.

Definition:
eWallet or E-wallet: An eWallet is a software program that stores a user's private keys which control the user's cryptocurrency.

Upon sending the transaction, the sender signs the transaction with his or her "private" key, known by no one else, similar to a password. The full nodes then check to make sure the transaction was properly signed and that the sender's wallet has enough coins to send the transaction to other full nodes who also verify. This transaction quickly spreads across the network until everyone knows about the transaction that originated from the sender's public address.

Note:
As more and more transactions are submitted, full nodes can become inundated with them!

To have their transactions processed quickly and moved closer to the front of the consensus line, users often pay a transaction fee to the full nodes to incentivize them and make the transaction an attractive choice. The consensus process is handled by a consensus algorithm, and one of its main purposes is to prevent a user from double spending.

Consensus Algorithms

There are three main consensus algorithms, and they are called: Proof of Importance, Proof of Stake and Proof of Work.

- **Proof of Importance**

  Proof of importance is a consensus algorithm introduced in early 2015. The algorithm determines which miner is most authorized to verify a transaction by assigning a degree of importance to the miner. The degree of importance isestablished by several factors, such as the length of time a miner has been part of the network, or how often other miners have accepted information generated by the miner as a measure of credibility.

- **Proof of Stake**

  This protocol states that a degree of authority is assigned to how many Bitcoins a miner owns, inferring that the more stake a miner has, or the more skin in the game, the more likely they are to be careful about analyzing transactions which could affect their own holdings. As the name indicates, the larger the stake a miner has in the system, the greater his or her importance. Essentially, the importance of a miner is subject to the amount of value they own.

- **Proof of Work**

  Proof of work refers to the data processing necessary to satisfy the algorithmic requirements of a block before the block can be verified and added to the blockchain. Proof of work requires resources that can be costly and time-consuming to produce, but which is easily verified once created.

Blocks

As you know by now, a block is a unit of data that is permanently recorded. Sometimes the data can be about transactions that have occurred, much like a record book shows the exchange of title and property over time, or a ledger that records stock transactions.

Blocks are linked sequentially in a chain called a blockchain. New transactions are grouped to create new blocks which contain about 800 transactions. The new blocks are added to the front of the chain once they have been verified by consensus. These blocks can never be altered or removed once they've been added to the network, though orphaned blocks can be removed by some software applications.

Note:
Each block contains about 800 – 1,000 transactions.

How Blocks Are Connected: Blocks are joined on the blockchain with links called hash that reference the preceding block. If the data in any previous block is changed, the hash changes, too, which breaks the authenticity of the chain and alerts participants that an error has occurred.

Here is an example of a hash:

```
0594A6E8F144755E5211F65DE7C9786FD685A20221BBECCCDA6B0055B9E4129B
```

Figure 5. Hash Example 1.

This is the hash for the name "Frank Roman", one of the contributors to this book. If you were to change the "F" to a lower case "frank Roman", the hash would change to this:

```
B10104FBB0DB5BB7E10AE5C6E31CEA2D48C539F0E2AD9BD8DE3F19F1983215CD
```

Figure 6. Hash Example 2.

You will notice that making even one small change to the hash generated a completely different hash, making a new digital fingerprint.

Nonce: A nonce is a 32-bit field composed of random numbers that can be used only once, and set so the block's hash will contain a sequence of leading zeros. Calculating the composition of the nonce according to the requirements is what takes so much time, computing resources, and results in the proof of work.

Time and Hashrate: A hashrate is the amount of attempts per second that a miner makes in trying to find a nonce that solves a block. The faster the hash rate, the better the opportunity that a miner will solve a block. On the Bitcoin network, there are currently about 20,000,000 TH/s. A TH/s is 1 trillion hashes per second...so that's a lot of computing every second of every day. The amount of energy consumed by this computing power is extravagant, and this is why miners will group together and pool their computing resources.

Note:

At the start of 2018 there were 508,195 Bitcoin blocks. Multiply this number by 1,000 and you'll approximate the number of Bitcoin transactions there were at this time.

Mining Profitability: When a block is solved and accepted by the blockchain network, a miner receives payment for the work performed. This payment is agreed-upon by all the nodes in the network. As of April 2018, each block generates 12.5 Bitcoins for the successful miner. In addition, the miner receives transaction fees paid by the users whose transactions were processed. As time goes by, payment in the form of new Bitcoins will no longer be available, as there are only a finite number of Bitcoins. Eventually, only transaction fees will be the incentive for miners to process transactions.

Scaling Problems

Because blockchains are composed of nodes that must each process every transaction, the size of the blockchain network can become cumbersome and create a lag in the processing and approval or rejection of new blocks. The benefits of the blockchain, which is security, authenticity of data, political neutrality, and the democratization of information without the control of a third party are a trade-off for the speed of transaction processing. The speed of the transaction processing is dependent not on the number of nodes but on the "block size limit", which is essentially the number of transactions that can fit into one block.

Note:
The total size of all the current Bitcoin data transactions as of 2018 was about 200 gigabytes.

Because there is no central authority, requiring nodes to make changes for the good of the network is not presently enforceable. The situation brings to a head the choice between rapid productivity from centralization versus low productivity and decentralization. Several possible solutions have been considered by the network, but there has been no consensual decision to date. For the time being, this problem remains.

Note:
If you trade bitcoins, your transactions are probably in many different blocks in the Bitcoin blockchain.

The Potential Danger: There is a potential danger for a cabal of powerful nodes to control the network. As the requirements for computing power increases, nodes with less resources may be forced to withdraw because of increased costs and the lack of profitability when competing against huge interests.

A Finite Number of Bitcoins: The number of bitcoins is finite. There will only ever be 21,000,000 of them. Once these 21 million have been created, mining will continue because of the need to process transactions, but then the only incentive will be to earn the transaction fees, not the ownership of newly mined Bitcoins.

Private Keys and Public Addresses

The choice of making information public or private is a consistent concern in our constantly evolving digital society. Security of our data is a primary issue as networks around the world grow tighter and more technologically advanced. Being able to protect the information you wish to keep private is paramount, and the commentary that follows demonstrates another method of how the blockchain system has remained tamper-proof, in this case through the application of private keys.

Private Keys and Public Keys

When people send you cryptocoins over the blockchain, they are actually sending them to a hashed version of what's known as the "public key". There is also another key, known as the "private key", which is hidden from view. The private key is used to derive the public key. You can know your own private key, and everyone else on the blockchain knows their own private key, but the private key should not be shared with others unless you want your cryptocurrencies stolen!

Key:
Always keep your private key private!

A private key is a secret, alphanumeric password/number used to spend/send your Bitcoins to another Bitcoin address. Both the private key and the public key are huge integer numbers, and since these numbers are so large, they are usually represented using a separate Wallet Import Format (WIF) also consisting of letters and numbers. It is a 256-bit long number which is picked randomly as soon as you make a wallet, and the private key always starts with the number 5. The degree of randomness and uniqueness is well defined by cryptographic functions for security purposes.

Definition:
Wallet Import Format (WIF): The WIF is the process for encoding a private key to make it easier to transmit on a blockchain.

```
5HueCGU8rMjxEXxiPuD5BDku4MkFqeZyd4dZ1jvhTVqvbTLvyTJ
```

Figure 7: Sample Private Key in Wallet Import Format (WIF)

The private key is the longer of the two, and is used to generate a signature for each blockchain transaction a user sends. This signature confirms the transaction has come from a specific user, and also prevents the transaction from being altered by anyone once it has been issued. In short, you sign the cryptocurrencies you send to others using a private key. If someone were to obtain your private key, they would be able to send your cryptocurrencies to themselves, verifying that transaction with your private key—in effect stealing from you!

Note:
Your private key is your signature of approval.

The private key is used to mathematically derive the public key, which includes information about the network and the amount of value being transferred. This information is then transformed with a hash function to produce the address that other people can see. You receive cryptocurrencies others send to your address, which is composed of the hash of your public key and other pertinent information.

Public Address

The public address is another alphanumeric address/number which is derived from private keys by using cryptographic math functions. The public address is used to publicly receive bitcoins and this is how a Bitcoin public address looks. It always starts with the number 1.

1EHNa6Q4Jz2uvNExL497mE43ikXhwF6kZm

The public address is always visible so it can be used to send and receive bitcoins.

Note:
Users can make as many public addresses as they wish to receive Bitcoins.

You may be wondering if a public key can be reversed through a generator to identify a private key, allowing the opportunity for theft, but cryptocurrencies solve this issue by using a complicated mathematical algorithm to generate the public keys. The algorithm makes it very easy to generate public keys from private keys, but extremely difficult to "reverse" the algorithm to reveal the private key.

The algorithm is extremely complex and involves converting the private key to a binary representation, identifying the bits in this binary representation that have a value of 1, and summing an exponentially multiplied generator variable to arrive at the final public key. Whew! This description of public key generation is a mouthful, but the process of reversing this calculation is even more complex—so much so that the world's most powerful computer would need more than 40,000,000, 000,000,000,000,000,000,000,000 years (that's 31 zeroes!) to complete the calculation.

So...could it be done? Yes.

Is it likely? Uh, no.

Summary

Cryptocurrency mining is a complex task, as you would imagine. Mining requires a huge amount of computer and electrical resources in order to encrypt, relay, and verify data in the blockchain. Though the system is currently cumbersome, particularly for its scalability, yet it assures the transfer of accurate data in a system that does not require centralized third-party supervision. Independence from central control is a key benefit for individuals choosing to engage in the block chain system.

Like everything else, it has its strong points and its vulnerabilities, but the exciting facet of cryptocurrency mining, private keys and public addresses is that it creates a new form of authentic wealth transference that can be applied to every or almost every facet of our continually and rapidly developing digitally-represented lives. Because of this, our society, our culture, and the world advances into the unknown, pioneering one more footstep into a future we may presently only dimly see.

Chapter 4: Review Questions

1. Miners compete against each other to solve for a nonce that creates a hash with the correct number of zeros for a block because:

A. They enjoy competition

B. The first miner to calculate the right hash is likely to be paid

C. Miners need the right hash to be a user

D. A miner's private key unlocks their public address

2. Today, mining requires access to limited computing power.

A. True

B. False

3. Anyone can be a user, but a node requires a high-speed broadband connection.

A. True

B. False

4. When a transaction is transmitted, the user:

a. Signs the transaction with a private key

b. Full nodes check the authenticity of the transaction

c. The user's wallet is checked to verify sufficient funds for the work

d. The entire network reviews the transaction and provides consensus or objects to the transaction

A. The correct sequence of events is a, b, c, d

B. The correct sequence of events is a, b, d, c

C. The correct sequence of events is a, c, b, d

D. The correct sequence of events is a, d, b, c

5. Proof of Importance states that a degree of authority of a miner is subject to the amount of currency the miner owns.

A. True

B. False

6. A block is:

A. A unit of nonce

B. A unit of currency

C. A unit of data

D. A unit of nodes

7. Miners are currently paid 12.5 Bitcoins for every block generated. In the future, payment in the form of new Bitcoins will no longer be available.

A. True

B. False

8. Is fraud possible on the Bitcoin blockchains?

A. Yes

B. No

9. A private key is generated from a public key.

A. True

B. False

10. You must never reveal your private key or:

    A. Your currency can be stolen

    B. You would change your public key information

    C. The public address will be confused with someone else

    D. Your public key will make your private key know and void

Chapter 4: Answers

1. Miners compete against each other to solve for a nonce that creates a hash with the correct number of zeros for a block because:

A. They enjoy competition

B. The first miner to calculate the right hash is likely to be paid

C. Miners need the right hash to be a user

D. A miner's private key unlocks their public address

Answer: B. A miner is only paid for their work if they are the first miner to calculate the correct hash for a block, there is consensus agreeing with the miner's proof-of-work, and other qualifications.

2. Today, mining requires access to limited computing power.

A. True

B. False

Answer: B. At one time a miner could mine with limited computing power, but today the algorithms are so complex that miners have to band together to combine computing resources so they can compete against server farms making rapid calculations.

3. Anyone can be a user, but a node requires a high-speed broadband connection.

A. True

B. False

Answer: A. True. Anyone who wants to be a user

on a blockchain network is likely to be permitted, but being a node requires a high-speed broadband connection for making the rapid calculations necessary to accept, validate, and relay transactions and blocks.

4. When a transaction is transmitted, the user:

a. Signs the transaction with a private key

b. Full nodes check the authenticity of the transaction

c. The user's wallet is checked to verify sufficient funds for the work

d. The entire network reviews the transaction and provides consensus or objects to the transaction

A. The correct sequence of events is a, b, c, d.

B. The correct sequence of events is a, b, d, c.

C. The correct sequence of events is a, c, b, d.

D. The correct sequence of events is a, d, b, c.

Answer: A. First the user signs the transaction and a hash is created, then the full nodes check the authenticity of the hash. After that, the user's wallet is verified for sufficient funds, and last of all the transaction is reviewed and confirmed.

5. Proof of Importance states that a degree of authority of a miner is subject to the amount of currency the miner owns.

A. True

B. False

Answer: B. False. Proof of Importance states a miner is reliable due to such factors as the length of time a minor has been part of the network, or how often other miners have accepted the miner's work as credible.

6. A block is:

A. A unit of nonce

B. A unit of currency

C. A unit of data

D. A unit of nodes

Answer: C. A block is a unit of data that is permanently recorded.

7. Miners are currently paid 12.5 Bitcoins for every block generated. In the future, payment in the form of new Bitcoins will no longer be available.

A. True

B. False

Answer: A. True. There are only a finite number of Bitcoins. Once all of the Bitcoins have been mined, a miner will only be awarded with transaction fees, and only if they are the successful miner on a transaction.

8. Is fraud possible on the Bitcoin blockchains?

A. Yes

B. No

Answer: A. Yes. Technology is still in its infancy, and there is always the possibility of more advanced technology supplanting existing technology. Also, it may be possible that a cabal could control the Bitcoin blockchain by gaining 51% of the blockchain network. Another hazard, though not a fraudulent one, is that blockchains are dependent on giant amounts of electrical power, so if the power sources failed, servers and computers would stop their calculations and the system's structure would collapse.

9. A private key is generated from a public key.

   A. True.

   B. False.

   Answer: B. False. The public key is available for everyone to see, but the private key is kept secret. The public key is generated from the private key.

10. You must never reveal your private key or:

   A. Your currency can be stolen

   B. You would change your public key information

   C. The public address will be confused with someone else

   D. Your public key will make your private key know and void

   Answer: A. Your private key is like your personal signature. If other people know it, they can use it to steal your currency or information.

Chapter 5

The Evolving Financial System by Eryka Gemma

Eryka Gemma is a well-known cryptocurrency expert. published author and professional speaker on digital assets and the decentralized ecosystem.

This chapter provides six insightful passages that explore contemporary regulatory challenges and technological advancements. Each passage offers a review and analysis of how these factors shape the future of digital assets and their adoption in global finance.

Objectives

In this chapter you will:

- Understand the differences between Web 1, Web 2, and Web 3, and how Web 3 serves the crypto ecosystem
- Become familiar with the concept of the CBDC, Central Bank Digital Currency, and decide if a CBDC is helpful or not
- Increase your awareness of the decentralized financial industry and your potential role within it
- Learn the details of crypto wallets and keys, and how they function

- Find out how crypto mining can reduce wasted resources

NFTs, Memes and the Metaverse: The Inevitability of a New Financial System

The timing of the “new year” has always seemed odd. One might expect a fresh start to align with spring — a season of rebirth and growth — rather than the dead of winter. Regardless of when we mark the beginning, one constant remains: cycles govern our world. History repeats itself. The role of an informed investor involves understanding how macro-level trends (where we are in the larger economic cycle) impact micro-level outcomes (a company’s likelihood of success). Let’s explore our current position in the cycle and what to expect as blockchain technology reshapes our financial landscape.

Recognizing Patterns of Change

Across various religions and ideologies, recurring themes of transformation emerge. Christians anticipate the “second coming of Christ.” Astrologers highlight the “Age of Aquarius,” historically linked to major power shifts. Academics cite the Strauss–Howe generational theory, which suggests we are in the “Fourth Turning,” a period of upheaval and rebirth.

These perspectives all converge on one idea: a fundamental cultural shift is underway. Technology is not only making these predictions possible but accelerating them.

Blockchain and the Evolution of Value: Blockchain is at the core of this transformation, enabling new ways to establish, store, and exchange value. Here are some ways in which blockchain supports or enhances several trending technological shifts.

NFTs and the Monetization of Art: Rare collectibles have always held value for those who appreciate them. In the Digital Age, ownership of these assets is now secured on a blockchain, significantly reducing counterfeiting. While some may struggle to understand why a .jpeg of an ape wearing pink fur and a diamond grill in its mouth was purchased for $460,000, the high valuation of art is nothing new. History repeats itself. Sentimental attachment and scarcity drive value, but digital collectibles offer more than traditional art — they generate income.

For centuries, artists have struggled to monetize their work. Musicians, painters, and other creatives often see only a fraction of their earnings due to intermediaries. Art galleries take around 50% of a sale, and many artists are only recognized posthumously. Imagine a system where an artist earns royalties every time their work is resold — forever. Even after their passing, their estate continues to benefit.

Consider a musician who receives automatic micropayments every time their song is played, eliminating the need for lengthy legal battles over royalties. Imagine a gamer who can trade in-game items for real-world currency. This is no longer hypothetical — blockchain-based startups are making it a reality.

Professional athletes experience intense financial highs and lows. In the NFL, 72% of players face financial distress within five years of retirement; the rate is 60% for the NBA, and MLB players are four times more likely to file for bankruptcy than the average American. Blockchain allows athletes to create and sell their own memorabilia, monetize their personal brand, and secure income beyond their playing years.

Social media has already decentralized entertainment, allowing creators to bypass traditional gatekeepers. However, platforms like YouTube impose restrictive monetization policies, forcing creators to self-censor to remain profitable. Web3 and blockchain-based micropayments are changing this landscape, enabling true creative freedom.

Until now, creatives have had little participation in the future earnings of their work. With NFTs and smart contracts, that infrastructure is being built. The long-term impact of this new incentive model is yet to be fully realized, but its potential is immense.

The Metaverse: A New Digital Reality

The concept of the metaverse has gained traction, especially with Facebook rebranding as "Meta" and committing billions of dollars to virtual-world development. But what is the metaverse? It's an online universe where virtual reality and digital assets converge. There will be multiple metaverses, each with its own avatars, currencies, and economies. The shift toward a "Ready Player One" society, where interactions occur primarily online, has only been accelerated by pandemic-induced lockdowns, youth trends and shifting consumer behaviors.

Let's connect the metaverse with NFTs. Take the Bored Ape Yacht Club (BAYC), one of the most prominent NFT collections. Owning a BAYC grants exclusive access to a digital clubhouse, where an API verifies ownership before entry. At its heights, the floor price to join this elite networking space was around $250,000 with names like Justin Bieber, Paris Hilton, Jimmy Fallon, and Kevin Hart.

In the metaverse, status is displayed not through Rolexes or private clubs but through digital avatars, virtual real estate, and exclusive online communities. Although the floor price of these apes have significantly fallen to about $30,000, the virtual access provided was much more innovative than in the traditional art space.

Blockchain has enabled digital scarcity, and virtual land sales are already happening. In November 2021, a plot of land in "Decentraland" sold for $2.4 million, highlighting a growing trend: real estate moguls are adding virtual properties to their portfolios.

While I personally prefer in-person interactions and find aspects of the metaverse unsettling, the decentralization of digital spaces offers individuals greater autonomy. With multiple metaverses emerging, blockchain is shifting power from centralized entities to individuals, allowing people to shape their own digital realities according to their preferences.

A New Financial Paradigm

Blockchain is redefining value exchange, ownership, and creativity.

We are entering an era where individuals — artists, athletes, gamers, and entrepreneurs — can reclaim control over their earnings and personal brands. The empowerment of the individual is no longer a distant dream; it is happening now. As we move through this inevitable transition, one thing is clear: history repeats itself, but this time, technology is ensuring that power is distributed more equitably than ever before.

Enter Meme Coins

I have monitored the trends in crypto over each cycle in the market. Each 'bull run" is marked by a new idea trading at ridiculous valuations. In the 2017 bull cycle, which can be categorized as Bitcoins Mainstream breakthrough, the idea was ICOs, Initial Coin Offerings, which can be described as a mix between crowd funding and IPOs.

With ICOs an investor could trade their Ethereum for a different coin that didn't necessarily represent equity in the project but was subject to price fluctuations based on the success of the project. Today, ICOs have mostly died with many failed projects due to lack of adoption and the US regulator passing out fines and labeling ICOs an unregulated security.

In the 2020-21 bull run which brought institutional adoption and highlighted the "Digital Gold" narrative, the big idea was NFTs, as explained in detail above. Although the concept and capabilities NFTs enable are grand, the use cases have not been widely adopted; in my opinion it is because NFTs will always be niche to an audience and should have always been treated as such. Paying $4.2M for a baseball card of Babe Ruth is something only baseball and collectible lovers can understand. There are creators who utilize NFTs to engage their audiences but they are usually the tech-forward creators.

In March 2021, Grimes, one of Elon Musk's ex-partners, sold out her NFT collection for a total $6M, with the most expensive piece selling at about $350K. What has this done for her fans who bought her virtual art? Well, the floor price for her pieces now range from $150 to $500 and she has stopped being a vocal advocate on the profitability of NFTs. The NFT market grew by 299% in 2020 and today it is a stain on the outsiders' perception of the digital asset industry.

So what's the trend of this current cycle? It is meme coins on Layer 1 chains like Solana, Ethereum and Coinbase's Base. The Friday before inauguration $Trump was released and hit an all-time high market cap of $12.8B with a price of $75 per coin within 24 hours. $Melania was released and reached a market cap of $734M. This was an act that provided a piece of regulatory clarity the industry so badly wanted. People knew for sure that their meme coins would not be prosecuted because the new president set a precedent.

But what are meme coins? Memetics is a field of study that explores the idea that cultural information, behaviors, and ideas can spread and evolve in a manner analogous to biological evolution. Meme coins have become a mix between the ICO era and NFTs, fixing key problems from each of its predecessors. ICOs had utility which made these tokens both a security and a problem to unaccredited investors in the United States. NFTs are illiquid; this scarcity adds value but limits its trading potential.

Meme coins are purely speculative; they are legally not allowed to have any utility, and the volatility of these coins is wild ... thousands of percent up and down within minutes. The way I like to describe meme coins is that they are like fashion on the blockchain. I cannot explain why someone would pay $2,300 for a Louis Vuitton bag made from canvas! This most popular bag isn't even made from leather, yet every other girl aspires to hold this as a piece in her closet. Why would someone spend hard-earned money to wear this bag on their shoulder? Because they want to. Because they want to be part of the club. Because they see this bag as beautiful. Nothing tangible, little hope for resale value, but just the feeling of status and a sense of belonging to an exclusive club.

In fashion, new brands entering the market often fail; rarely do you see a new brand make it to the scale of Prada or Chanel. In memes, a lot of the coins fail to garnish the attention and market cap needed to sustain long-term value. In fashion, there are counterfeits, frauds and fast fashion clothes. In memes there are a lot of scams and counterfeits trying to trick people into buying the wrong thing. Fashion trends change and clothes go out of style. For memes, what's popular changes and memes that were once popular shift. They are purely speculative with the potential of becoming extremely liquid by touching global audiences.

Connecting with a meme name or idea earlier than everyone else is like the hope of being early to a fashion trend, except in memes there's hope for resale value.

Be very careful in the meme coin markets! When people show interest in this blockchain enabled market, the first question I ask is if they prefer roulette or blackjack.

Back to Basics Bitcoin: A Financial Revolution

Money is built on a shared belief system — its value depends on collective trust. When that trust erodes, history has shown that economic, political, and social upheavals follow.

Though blockchain technology is new, the reset it represents is not. History repeats itself. The founding of America was driven by the decentralization of knowledge. With the invention of the printing press, the Bible was mass-produced for the first time. Regardless of religious belief, the Bible undeniably asserts that individual rights are granted by a higher power, not by the state. When the people of Great Britain realized their religious leaders had misled them, they grew frustrated with oppressive taxes, and, understanding their inalienable rights, the boldest among them sought a New World.

Today, in 2025, we are once again on the verge of discovery — this time, an individual journey fueled by decentralized knowledge. The truth about excessive government spending and financial instability is available to those willing to confront and understand it. Those who seek solutions will emerge as leaders in this new era where sound money is no longer dictated by governments but secured by a public ledger, a network of computers, and mathematical certainty.

The Inevitable Shift

History moves in cycles — there is nothing new under the sun. As the pendulum swings and surveillance with technology expands, we find ourselves facing new heights of government overreach and control. Yet history has also proven that human ingenuity always finds a way forward. Today's pursuit of freedom has enabled people to bypass traditional gatekeepers and harness collective knowledge. Blockchain technology takes this dynamic further, allowing trustless, global interaction at an unprecedented scale.

It's clear that our current financial expansion is unsustainable. The Federal Reserve's relentless quantitative easing (QE), combined with record-breaking government spending, has drastically inflated the money supply (M2). Historically, fiat currencies last about 35 years on average — the U.S. dollar, in its unbacked form, is now over 50. Those who have been paying attention saw the warning signs long ago and have built an alternative financial system. The ship appears to be sinking, and while the masses may be powerless to stop it, the strongest lifeboat we have is cryptocurrency.

Some may interpret these events through different lenses – spiritual, economic, or historical – but the pattern remains the same. We are in a phase of reset, whether we accept it or not. The collapse of the old system is inevitable, but so is the rise of something new and exciting.

Our choice is simple but not easy: fear the unknown or embrace the future.

Decentralized Finance: Breaking the Lending Frontier

The invention of Bitcoin has opened Pandora's box, marking just the beginning of a financial revolution. Blockchain technology is rapidly transforming traditional financial structures, taking programmable money to an entirely new level.

What is DeFi?

DeFi, short for Decentralized Finance, is a blockchain-based financial system that replaces traditional banking activities with automated software. It allows individuals to manage their assets without intermediaries, giving them full control over their finances.

With DeFi, users can trade, lend, and borrow money through open-source protocols while maintaining ownership of their assets. DeFi removes the chance of human error, bias, and the need for salaries cutting into profit margins.

This is in stark contrast to traditional banking, where institutions make money by lending, borrowing, and trading among themselves — often at the expense of depositors.

The Problem with Traditional Banking

Banks profit enormously from lending out deposits, but they don't share those profits with account holders. Consider this:

- Since March 2020, fractional reserve regulations have allowed banks to hold zero physical cash for every $100 deposited.
- This means banks can lend out your money indefinitely, making massive profits while you earn almost nothing.
- As of October 2021, the average savings account interest rate was just 0.06% APY, while banks continue to generate significant returns.

How DeFi Changes the Game

In a DeFi system, depositors can earn significantly higher returns — typically between 2% to 20% APY. Additionally, users can:

- Borrow funds without credit checks by posting collateral.
- Trade, lend, and borrow assets while keeping control of their private keys, thanks to smart contracts.

Unlike traditional banks, DeFi operates transparently without having to pay the salaries of gate keepers, ensuring that profits and opportunities are more equitably distributed.

DeFi's Explosive Growth

The rise of DeFi in 2020 revolutionized the crypto industry, leading to the creation of innovative financial protocols.

- Total Locked Value (TLV) — the amount of digital assets secured in DeFi smart contracts — has skyrocketed:
    - January 2020: $600 million
    - January 2025: $241 billion (a 400x increase in under five years)

This value is used to provide liquidity for trading, borrowing, minting assets, and even insuring both digital and real-world products. By locking cryptocurrencies into DeFi protocols, users can earn compounding interest at significantly higher rates than traditional banks offer.

Why DeFi Has Massive Potential

DeFi presents a low-risk, high-yield opportunity for growing savings, particularly for those seeking stable and scalable strategies. The introduction of stablecoins has further reduced volatility, making DeFi attractive even to institutional investors.

While DeFi is still a new financial tool and may seem complex, it has already demonstrated its ability to generate consistent returns, reduce capital restrictions, and provide transparent financial services. As adoption continues, DeFi is set to reshape how individuals and institutions interact with money — ushering in a more inclusive, decentralized, and profitable financial future.

A New Use Case for the Internet: Web 3

When the Internet became publicly available in August 1991, few could have predicted how essential it would become. Now, 34 years later, it is deeply embedded in our daily lives. Although its true value comes from the people who contribute content, many of these individuals are not directly or properly compensated for their contributions.

Like all technology, the Internet has evolved through distinct phases, adapting to new innovations. We are now entering its next major transformation, commonly known as Web 3. To fully grasp its significance, let's first look at the Internet's previous stages.

The Evolution of the Internet

Web 1: The Static Web: "Read Only"

The first phase of the internet, known as Web 1, was characterized by simple, static web pages — mostly personal websites hosted on ISP-run servers or free hosting platforms. Content was stored directly within the website's files, limiting how much information could be shared. The design was heavily reliant on HTML, often using tables and frames — practices now considered outdated.

Examples of Web 1 include early platforms like MySpace, LiveJournal, and Xanga where users could create basic personal pages. These websites lacked interactivity, meaning user engagement was minimal.

Web 2: The Social Media Era: "Read and Write"

In the late 1990s and early 2000s, the Internet transitioned to Web 2, introducing a more interactive, user-driven experience. This era, known as the "social media era," saw the rise of user-generated content such as:

- Social media posts (Facebook, Twitter, Instagram)
- Product reviews (Amazon, Yelp)
- Wiki contributions (Wikipedia)
- Blog comments and editorial input

With Web 2, the barrier to entry was significantly lowered as anyone with Internet access could participate, even without technical knowledge. Static websites were replaced by dynamic, interactive platforms that emphasized user experience and relied on APIs, allowing seamless integration of third-party applications.

One defining characteristic of Web 2 is data monetization. Many of the largest companies in the world — often referred to as FAANG (Facebook, Apple, Amazon, Netflix, Google) — offer "free" services, but they make billions of dollars by collecting and selling user data. In return, users receive nothing but likes and follows while corporations profit from their online activities without compensation.

Web 3: The Next Evolution: "Read, Write ... and Own"

Now, we are entering Web 3, a shift that empowers individuals to monetize their own data and creative contributions. Built on principles of decentralization, openness, and greater user control, Web 3 introduces blockchain technology to store data across multiple locations simultaneously instead of relying on a single centralized server.

In contrast to Web 2, where corporations control data and profit from it, Web 3 is trustless and permissionless — meaning anyone can access content without relying on gatekeepers. We are already seeing its implementation in Decentralized Finance (DeFi) applications such as:

- Uniswap – A decentralized exchange allowing users to swap and stake cryptocurrencies without intermediaries.
- NFTs (Non-Fungible Tokens) – A Web 3 innovation enabling content creators to monetize their work independently, ensuring continued earnings and ownership rights.

With NFTs, artists, musicians, and writers can earn royalties indefinitely, as ownership is recorded on the blockchain. Unlike traditional servers that can crash and evaporate all stored content, blockchain technology ensures that as long as there are network participants, content remains accessible.

The Future of Web 3

Though Web 3 is still in its early stages, its impact is already evident. As of now:

- The market cap of all cryptocurrencies sits at $3.16 trillion
- DeFi Total Value Locked (TVL) sits at $207 billion.

However, we are just beginning to unlock the full potential of Web 3. Imagine a future where:

- Every “like” on social media earns you micropayments.
- Users cannot be de-platformed for expressing different viewpoints because they own their data.

- Artists' families continue to receive royalties from their work, generation after generation.
- Journalists earn directly from reader engagement, eliminating the need for centralized media gatekeepers.

While many people today demand equality, Web 3 proposes a solution where fair compensation is embedded into the system itself. Rather than relying on corporations or governments to dictate fairness, Web 3 programs economic incentives directly into its protocols.

The Internet has always been a tool for innovation and disruption. Web 3 represents the next step — one where individuals regain control, ownership, and financial rewards for their contributions. The challenges will change, but so will the solutions. The future is just beginning.

A Central Bank Digital Currency (CBDC): Monetary Evolution or Financial Tyranny?

Bitcoin is an invention streamlining the way we exchange value. Its open-source nature allows the source code to be peer-reviewed, copied, and modified by anyone who desires to do so. The industry has named Bitcoin's underlying technology as "blockchain," with many companies taking the original code and modifying it to fit their business use cases. Companies such as IBM, Microsoft, Accenture, Mastercard, and Visa each have patents on blockchain technology.

While the merits of a blockchain can be disputed based on its level of decentralization and the security of its network, the idea of a distributed database that verifies itself via a math-based ledger has sparked major interest globally — especially by central bankers in charge of our money. A widely disputed use case for blockchain comes in the form of CBDCs or Central Bank Digital Currencies. Essentially, CBDCs are purely digital currencies issued by central banks. They can be used internally to help interbank settlements and externally to distribute to the retail market.

In an October 2020 Goldman Sachs report titled *What's in Store for the Dollar*, a CBDC is defined as "a new form of money, issued digitally by the central bank and intended to serve as legal tender. From an accounting perspective, it is a third form of liability for the central bank, alongside cash and central bank reserves." The report details the efforts and progress of sixteen different countries in developing CBDCs. According to Sachs, "CBDCs are coming; it's just a question of when."

The Bank of International Settlements (BIS) published a white paper in 2017 titled CBDC - *Central Bank Digital Currencies: Foundational Principles and Core Features*. This 26-page document, written by the central bank of central banks, explains how a CBDC can "provide a complementary central bank money to support a more resilient and diverse domestic payment system, offering opportunities not possible with cash while supporting innovation."

It's easy to argue that our money is already digital, with only 8% of the world's currency in physical cash. With COVID-19 coin shortages, entire countries eliminating cash, and rewards for swiping cards, it's clear that a cashless society is already in motion.

So, what's the big deal about a CBDC? Ah! Here it is: it uses a private blockchain. The Bitcoin blockchain is an open blockchain, allowing anyone to contribute work to verify the validity of the ledger. This makes politically neutral, uncensorable value transfer possible. A private blockchain, however, is a closed system with minimal participants in charge of approving transactions. It is a fancy database that piggybacks on the merits of Bitcoin, exploiting the masses' misunderstanding of technology. CBDCs will operate on private blockchains, in other words, out of the control of regular people and yet another way of controlling the exchange of money and value.

Think about the following scenario: Every single person receives a unique wallet address to receive funds. People will be incentivized to obtain this wallet address through monetary rewards, forcing compliance with strenuous Know Your Customer (KYC) banking requirements. By doing so, each person creates a digital identity tied to their wallet. Every transaction spent from this wallet becomes traceable by those who control the private blockchain ledger, painting a detailed picture of an individual's spending habits and business relationships. Wallets can easily be flagged and tagged with an approval rating based on spending habits. Is this healthy? No!

The level of control this brings to central bankers is dystopian. They will have the ability to intervene directly in every transaction in the economy. Removing an individual from the financial system becomes easier than ever before, and questioning the official story could lead to losing access to your funds. Every dollar will be accounted for, and the central bank must consent to every transaction. Blockchain introduces a level of information storage and ease of distribution never before possible in dealing with money. This opens the door to a tyrannical system.

As talks of a Universal Basic Income and additional stimulus checks increase, so does the necessity of a CBDC to ease fund distribution. Patents are already in place to facilitate cryptocurrency distribution. In March 2020, Microsoft filed patent no. 2020060606 — yes, Patent 666 — which references a sensory device that reads body data and rewards users in cryptocurrency for performing certain tasks. It makes you wonder: What kind of tasks deserve a reward according to corporate thinking? Just guess!

Some draw parallels to the Bible's last book of Revelation and the "mark of the beast":

"It also forced all people, great and small, rich and poor, free and slave, to receive a mark on their right hands or on their foreheads, so that they could not buy or sell unless they had the mark, which is the name of the beast or the number of its name. This calls for wisdom. Let the person who has insight calculate the number of the beast, for it is the number of a man. That number is 666." - Revelation 13:16

This implementation of a "beast system" transcends speculation. Even if you don't believe in the Bible, concerns about surveillance and loss of autonomy are legitimate. On October 19, 2020, the International Monetary Fund streamed a meeting titled *Cross-Border Payment - A Vision for the Future.* BIS General Manager Agustin Carstens said, "The key difference of the CBDC is that central banks will have absolute control on the rules and regulations that will determine the use of that expression of central bank liability and also, we will have the technology to enforce that." Again, central bank control may not be in the best interests of the people.

In the recordings, Federal Reserve Chairman Jerome Powell discusses a Digital ID, citing "inclusion" and helping "poor people" obtain reliable national ID systems. Efficiency, inclusion, and diversity are repeatedly mentioned, alongside opportunities for emerging markets. However, money has always been a tool for control, and with blockchain, control has become greatly more efficient.

While we were distracted by COVID-19, election fraud, and 2020's riots, the foundation of commerce has been rocked. The money system is changing right under our noses. While CBDCs present opportunities, we must demand governance and transparency from central bankers in implementing blockchain technology. This uphill battle requires knowledge by the people and their focused will to act.

The people's true power is in having alternatives to CBDCs for transactions, especially for those who understand the dangers of centralized control. Although blockchain is being used to implement CBDCs, Bitcoin itself stands as the antithesis to this system. Bitcoin's network is transparent, rooted in sound monetary principles, and decentralized. It is a system no single entity controls, ensuring uncensorable transactions.

Bitcoin is not just an investment; it is a PARALLEL SYSTEM allowing individuals to transact financial activities when cash is eliminated and CBDCs are implemented.

A Timeline of Key CBDC Developments

In April 2023, "CBDC" began trending on Twitter, largely due to Robert F. Kennedy Jr.'s presidential campaign announcement, which highlighted concerns about the potential dangers of central bank digital currencies (CBDCs). Those who have followed the evolution of blockchain's open-source technology have seen this unfolding for years. A timeline of notable events in the CBDC category follows, complete with links for further exploration. It is crucial, nay, urgent, to spread awareness of these developments, and I appreciate the opportunity to share this information with you.

July 2021 – The U.S. House of Representatives held a hearing titled *The Promises and Perils of Central Bank Digital Currencies*. The discussion covered varying perspectives, with Congressman Andy Barr of Kentucky warning that CBDCs could bypass the private banking system.

https://www.congress.gov/event/117th-congress/house-event/LC67455/text

October 2021 – The G7 published *Public Policy Principles for Retail Central Bank Digital Currencies*, addressing financial stability, cybersecurity, privacy, inclusion, and energy efficiency.

https://www.gov.uk/government/publications/g7-public-policy-principles-for-retail-central-bank-digital-currencies-and-g7-finance-ministers-and-central-bank-governors-statement-on-central-bank

November 2021 – A report was released from the White House called *Report on Stable Coins*, created by the Presidents Working Group on Financial Markets, the FDIC and the OCC. Stable coins are indispensable in the crypto landscape because they represent fiat currency. The most popular US stable coin is Tether (USDT), created in 2014 with a current market cap of $81.8 billion and daily volume of $14B in size. Can you see why the Treasury department wants to require all stable coins to be government-run?

https://home.treasury.gov/system/files/136/StableCoinReport_Nov1_508.pdf

January 2022 – The Federal Reserve released *Money and Payments: The U.S. Dollar in the Age of Digital Transformation*, calling CBDCs the "safest form of money" but warning that they could reduce banking deposits. The potential centralization of funds in the Federal Reserve could undermine local banks, making them less of a priority in people's lives. How will this reduction in local banks' operations and influence change the daily financial activities of people?

https://www.federalreserve.gov/publications/money-and-payments-discussion-paper.htm

and:

https://www.federalreserve.gov/releases/h41/

March 2022 – President Biden signed an executive order prioritizing CBDC development and international promotion while increasing regulatory scrutiny on cryptocurrencies.

https://www.whitehouse.gov/briefing-room/statements-releases/2022/03/09/fact-sheet-president-biden-to-sign-executive-order-on-ensuring-responsible-innovation-in-digital-assets/

June 2022 – The Federal Reserve published public comments in its January 2022 report, *Money and Payments: The U.S. Dollar in the Age of Digital Transformation.* Concerns included privacy risks, potential financial disruptions, government overreach, and susceptibility to cyberattacks. Many fear that CBDCs could be weaponized against political dissenters. Why would anyone think THAT?

https://www.federalreserve.gov/cbdc-public-comments.htm

September 2022 – The Bank for International Settlements (BIS) declared a successful CBDC pilot, transacting $22 million among central banks in China, UAE, Hong Kong, and Thailand.

https://cointelegraph.com/news/bis-marks-cbdc-pilot-as-successful-with-

22m-transacted

September 2022 – The U.S. Treasury released *The Future of Money and Payments Report*, recommending continued research on a U.S. CBDC.

https://home.treasury.gov/system/files/136/Future-of-Money-and-Payments.pdf

March 2023 – The BIS concluded Project Icebreaker, a pilot between BIS Innovation Hub Nordic Centre, Bank of Israel, Norges Bank, and Sveriges Riksbank. What's interesting about Project Icebreaker is that it tests a "specific way to interlink domestic systems", that specific way being the exploration of how "retail CBDCs" can be spent. In contrast to FedNow which is product for banks, Project Icebreaker is foreshadowing the next step in this exploration – use by the common people.

https://www.bis.org/about/bisih/topics/cbdc/icebreaker.htm

July 2023 – The Federal Reserve launched *FedNow*, an instant payment service facilitating 24/7 bank transfers. While not a CBDC, it is seen as a foundational step for future CBDC deployment.

October 2023 – At the G20 Summit, nations emphasized CBDC interoperability for global trade and remittances, marking progress in international collaboration.

December 2023 – The European Central Bank moved to the pilot phase of the Digital Euro, testing integration with commercial banks and retail systems.

May 2024 – The U.S. House of Representatives passed H.R. 5403, also known as the CBDC Anti-Surveillance State Act. The bill aims to restrict the Federal Reserve from issuing a central bank digital currency (CBDC) without explicit authorization from Congress. Sponsored by Congressman Tom Emmer, the legislation emphasizes preserving financial privacy and preventing government overreach in the implementation of a digital dollar. While the bill passed the House, it has yet to be approved by the Senate, leaving its future uncertain.

https://financialservices.house.gov/news/documentsingle.aspx?DocumentID=409278#:~:text=5403%2C%20the%20CBDC%20Anti%2DSurveillance,without%20explicit%20authorization%20from%20Congress

November 2024 – Japan launched a full-scale pilot for the Digital Yen, selecting banks, fintech firms, and retailers to test its use in real-world transactions.

January 2025 – The new administration has taken a hard stance against CBDC's. On January 23, 2025, President Donald Trump signed Executive Order 14178, titled *"Strengthening American Leadership in Digital Financial Technology."* This order effectively revokes Executive Order 14067, issued on March 9, 2022, as well as the Department of the Treasury's *"Framework for International Engagement on Digital Assets,"* which had been released on July 7, 2022.

A key component of this new executive order is its prohibition on the establishment, issuance, or promotion of Central Bank Digital Currencies (CBDCs). The administration has expressed concerns that CBDCs could pose risks to financial stability, individual privacy, and national sovereignty, prompting the move to block their development.

This support for public blockchains and the references to fair banking services make it seem that the administration is opening the US borders for business.

Global Overview

CBDC exploration has surged, with 134 countries (representing 98% of global GDP) investigating CBDCs. 66 nations are in advanced stages, including 19 G20 countries. China's digital yuan (e-CNY) has processed nearly 7 trillion yuan in transactions.

Reality Check: With only 8% of the world's currency in physical cash, the transition to a digital economy is already underway. The U.S. faced (again) an impending debt ceiling suspension in January 2025, which heightened financial uncertainties. Governments have previously weaponized financial systems via sanctions; CBDCs could extend such control to individuals.

Prediction: My prediction is the distribution will happen through 'free money' from the government. About 30-40% of America's GDP is government spending; think about all the Covid-era stimulus and welfare checks that could easily have been distributed via CBDC. Consider how low interest rates have been in the last several years; what would happen if only assets held in CBDC would be able to earn interest?

CBDCs pose risks, including:

- **Privacy concerns** – Government surveillance and data access.
- **Centralized monetary policy** – Reduced local financial autonomy.
- **Cybersecurity threats** – Increased hacking vulnerabilities.

What Can Be Done?

- **Contact your representatives** – Several Congressional bills may restrict CBDC implementation.
- **Support legislation** – Congressman Tom Emmer introduced the CBDC *Anti-Surveillance State Act,* preventing the Federal Reserve from using a CBDC to control the economy. Show your support for him and other Congressional leaders supporting this Act. Contact:

  https://emmer.house.gov/

  https://www.congress.gov/get-alerts
- State-level action – Governor **Ron DeSantis** has proposed banning CBDCs in Florida. Show your support for DeSantis in this regard. Contact: https://www.flgov.com/eog/leadership/people/ron-desantis/contact The discussion around CBDCs is far from over. Awareness and advocacy are essential for shaping the future of digital finance. While I commend DeSantis's efforts, implementing such measures will be challenging due to the deeply interconnected nature of the nation's banking system. As Mayer Amschel Rothschild famously stated, "*Let me issue and control a nation's money, and I care not who writes the laws.*"

Warn Your Friends and Family

If a Central Bank Digital Currency (CBDC) is integrated into the financial system, avoiding its use will be extremely difficult. Especially now that there has been public outcry against CBDCs, it seems they may be taking on a new form in stablecoins. Although it is unknown exactly how this application of digital currency will take place, awareness is key — we can at least inform our loved ones about the potential implications and possibilities of privately issued blockchain based value transfer.

Stay Decentralized: Store Your Digital Assets in Cold Storage

The ongoing banking crises are designed to instill fear in local and small banks, but it is crucial to strengthen these institutions and embrace decentralized currencies. Bitcoin, rooted in transparency, sound monetary principles, and decentralization, offers an alternative financial system. Since no single entity controls its network, transactions remain uncensorable, providing your own personal control over your assets.

Maintaining financial sovereignty and transacting within a trustless economy is vital for those who question the official narrative and reject the imposition of a CBDC. Bitcoin is more than just an investment — again, it is a PARALLEL FINANCIAL SYSTEM that enables individuals to operate outside centralized monetary control.

Stay Informed

Continuously monitor official sources for the latest developments on CBDCs and related technologies. Here are two valuable resources:

- CBDC Tracker: https://cbdctracker.org/
- Atlantic Council CBDC Tracker: https://www.atlanticcouncil.org/cbdctracker/

Evaluate Financial Decisions

Consider how emerging digital currencies might impact your personal finances and investment strategies. When necessary, seek guidance from financial professionals to understand and interact in this evolving ecosystem effectively. I would exercise caution now that the term "CBDC" has been officially blacklisted. It's possible that stablecoins or other forms of "official blockchain money" could emerge, performing the same functions as a CBDC without being labeled as one.

Most of all ... Take action or accept the consequences of inaction!

The Private Keys of Wealth Preservation

Also discussed: The portability of Bitcoin, brain wallets, and crossing international borders with your wealth intact

Crossing borders with your wealth intact is a difficult feat for those whose wealth exceeds the legal limits. U.S. Customs allows international travel with only $10,000 undeclared. (Other countries have different allowable amounts.) This includes:

- Coins and banknotes, both domestic or foreign
- Gold coins (bullion will not count toward the U.S. customs cash limit but must still be declared)
- Travelers' checks
- Money orders
- Personal checks, cashier's checks, business checks
- Securities or stocks in bearer form
- Checks or money orders made out to someone other than the bearer that are endorsed without restriction (i.e., for deposit only)

- Incomplete checks, money orders, promissory notes that are signed but on which the name of the payee has been omitted (i.e., the "To" line is left blank)

(Source: https://clearitusa.com/u-s-customs-cash-limit/)

If you travel with more than the legal limit without declaration, Customs promises to "certainly have it seized from you" with no direct recourse to have it returned. Offenders of this rule are subject to a fine of up to $500,000 or 10 years in prison.

There is always the option to declare your finances by filling out FinCEN Form 105, a *Report of International Transportation of Currency or Monetary Instruments*. However, who wants to carry around that much cash or gold? Declaring you have these assets in your physical possession puts a huge target on your back.

For the ultra-wealthy, their banks can supply cross-border wealth advisory, but what if you don't have access to these resources? What if you are unable to access your national bank from another country? What if you are in a refugee situation where you must flee your home? What if you value privacy and simply don't want to disclose personal information?

A Trustless System

Traditional banking systems are archaic with frameworks created during a time when international travel was less accessible and people were meant to keep their money local. However, the biggest problem the traditional banking system faces is that it is completely built on trust -- you must trust in humans, you must trust unelected central bankers, you must trust that your bank will allow you to move your money when you please, and you must trust the government in which your fiat is denominated.

Although there are cross-border wealth preservation strategies, technology has provided a simple and advanced solution that allows you to access your wealth with just a cellphone, Wi-Fi signal, and your private keys. In this system you no longer have to trust because now you can verify there is no backdoor accessing your funds.

Bitcoin provides many benefits: privacy, unconfiscatability, sovereignty, security, transparency, durability, all in a trustless environment and built with sound money principles in mind. For this article, we are going to focus on just one aspect of bitcoin - its portability.

To truly take advantage of bitcoin's portability, you must hold your own "private keys". Although you may have bought bitcoin, holding it in a third party system like an exchange subjects you to a trust dependent system similar to banks. Simply put - not your keys: not your coins.

What Is a Private Key?

When you create a "wallet" on the bitcoin blockchain you are creating an "address", digital real estate where others can be directed to send you coins or receive your coins. Each wallet includes a "public key" and "private key". A public key can be treated just like it was the address to your email account. You can send and receive email with anyone who also has an email address. A private key can be treated as the key to your mailbox. You never share it because with this key you are able to access and remove the contents of your mailbox. A public key encrypts, while a private key decrypts. These keys are mathematically linked to one another and are the basis of asymmetric cryptography.

Public keys are also referred to as wallet addresses. Private keys are also referred to as seed or mnemonic phrases. A seed or mnemonic phrase is your private key encoded into 12 - 24 words so the user can more easily remember the code.

Public Key (35 characters):

1F3aK8hT2Mz6VqX9NwYpB4RcD7J5LZQoKm

Private Key (35 characters):

5J3bL9XyVwNz8QmT2FKa6R7D4Cp1MZBhGo

Mnemonic Seed Phrase (24 words):

clutch captain shoe salt awake harvest setup primary inmate ugly among become cash deposit fold silk hover cargo bike maximum load pepper lottery panel

These are randomly generated examples and should not be used for real transactions.

Figure 8: Examples of a Public Key, Private Key, and a Mnemonic or Seed Phrase.

A seed phrase is your password to access your wallet on the Bitcoin blockchain. If your computer or phone is damaged, you can upload this seed phrase using a different device and regain access to your wallet. These phrases must be kept with EXTREME care because if you lose the code, you will lose access to your wallet and there is no third party to help you recover your assets.

The beauty of private keys is that the keyholder is in ultimate control. There is no back door, no ability to freeze contents, and conversely, nobody to call on if you lose them. Personal accountability is a lost virtue with our money since we have depended on banks and FDIC insurance for so many decades. With bitcoin, we now have the ability to store wealth in our brains or on a piece of paper by knowing the 12 - 24 word seed phrase. The phrase is not tied to a single device, entity or even bitcoin wallet provider; it is your password for direct access to the Bitcoin blockchain ledger where your wealth is confirmed.

Wealth Preservation and Storage

What does this mean for crossing international borders? Or for the potential collapse of the fiat banking system? It means you can create a virtual address for your wealth to which only you have access; nobody else has to even know you own this property. You now can be your own Swiss bank account. This ability to store your wealth in a sovereign manner is not afforded via any other solutions. You can lose all your physical possessions ... but by remembering your private key, you know your wealth is safely stored on the blockchain.

Bitcoin provides virtual possibilities that are physically impossible with gold or cash.

Some have asked me, "What if an EMP (electromagnetic pulse) goes off and all power is lost?" If all power is lost, you have much bigger problems ... including the inaccessibility of all the money in your fiat bank account. With bitcoin, there are nodes stored all over the world which contain a copy of the Bitcoin ledger AND there is a Bitcoin node on a satellite in space. The effort to keep Bitcoin as decentralized as possible adds a superior level of protection in case catastrophic natural disasters destroy an area. This is much safer than data centers or "the cloud" which are physical walls of computers centrally located storing mass amounts of global information.

Jim Cramer of CNBC's *Mad Money* program has stated he likes bitcoin because it is native to his children's generation and "what if they forget where I hid the gold?" There are many creative ways to store your seed phrase to ensure your loved ones have access if needed.

Many great inventions can be identified by providing an improvement to the quality of life and the interconnectivity of individuals. With Bitcoin designed as a peer-to-peer cash system, the innovations that occur by cutting out the middlemen of banks are dynamic and still being discovered. One can only speculate what can happen when our money is no longer restricted to 9-5 banking hours, capital controls, the whims of the federal reserve, or the bank's business model of taking a piece of every transaction. We can only guess what will happen economically when 50% of the world's population who don't have access to a bank account can now transact globally with just a cellphone and Wi-Fi signal.

Bitcoin provides virtual possibilities that are physically impossible with gold or cash because it is the ultimate portable wealth storage method, especially for those who understand the technology's value proposition and are aware of and concerned about the state of our current and future global economy.

Green Energy, Satoshi's Second Gift

Oil and Gas Miners Become More Efficient Mining for Bitcoin

One of Bitcoin's most repeated criticisms is due to its large energy consumption. Running, validating, and securing the blockchain requires a lot of computational energy but so does watching Netflix. The difference between Netflix and adding hash power to bitcoin are the incentives. It has been said that Satoshi's second gift is green energy because bitcoin provides real incentives for individuals to find a more efficient use of power. This incentive has created vertical innovation in legacy industries like oil and gas.

Where there was once waste, there is now efficient power consumption upholding a global financial system.

The oil and gas industry is one of the largest contributors to greenhouse gas emissions due to oil rigs accidentally hitting natural gas reserves while drilling for oil. For years, the oil and gas industry has struggled to find solutions to this natural gas situation. Oil can be easily stored and transported but gas requires a pipeline, often not financially viable to build. As a result, the gas is released into an atmosphere or "flared", a pleasant way to say that it's burned-off. For oil and gas companies, this is quite literally, burning money.

Modern problems require modern solutions, and many crypto entrepreneurs have decided to find such solutions. In January 2019, two prep school pals from Denver drove out to the snow-covered plains of Wyoming where they built a machine intended to harness the "waste gas" from oil rigs to power cryptocurrency mining. Their company has since attracted high-profile investors, including Bain and Winklevoss Capital. Trademarking the solution as "digital flare mitigation", from the outside this looks like data centers housed inside structures placed onsite at remote oil rigs. The producers of oil are now:

1. Earning newly minted bitcoin or energy arbitrage income in place of the once-wasted natural gas

2. Reducing their carbon footprint

3. Contributing to the security of the Bitcoin blockchain

The process reduces CO2-equivalent emissions by about 63% compared with flaring, according to research from Denver-based Crusoe Energy Systems.

This is a fascinating time for both oil and Bitcoin industries, as the old and the new are working together in a symbiotic relationship. Bitcoin miners are using affordable natural gas to power their mining, and oil companies are no longer wasting a useful resource.

This partnership is still in its early stages, yet has already seen support from US lawmakers. In the 2022 Texas Blockchain Summit, Ted Cruz pointed out that the vast renewable energy produced in the south-central region of the U.S. was a great opportunity for Bitcoin miners: *"Texas has a lot of energy. Fifty percent of the natural gas in this country that is flared, is being flared in the Permian right now in West Texas. I think that is an enormous opportunity for Bitcoin because that is energy that is just being wasted."* The door is wide open for tapping into this emerging opportunity with support from lawmakers and oil companies benefitting from Bitcoin miners stationed at their rigs.

In mid-February 2022, one of the world's largest independent oil and gas exploration companies, ConocoPhillips, disclosed it has been selling excess gas to Bitcoin miners instead of burning it off. This is a trend that is likely continue to grow as oil and gas companies see the monetary opportunity, and as bitcoin miners seek cheaper sources of energy.

Before Bitcoin there were few incentives, aside from tax breaks, for an individual to dedicate time to creating and implementing green energy solutions. Now, bitcoin miners all over the world, eager to keep costs low, are innovating and using resources that would otherwise be wasted.

References:

https://zycrypto.com/120b-oil-and-gas-giant-conocophillips-joins-the-bitcoin-mining-fuel-business/

https://www.cnbc.com/2022/02/12/23-year-old-texans-made-4-million-mining-bitcoin-off-flared-natural-gas.html

https://www.cnbc.com/2022/02/15/conocophillips-is-selling-extra-gas-to-bitcoin-miners-in-north-dakota.html

https://zycrypto.com/senator-ted-cruz-believes-excess-renewable-energy-in-texas-presents-a-great-opportunity-for-bitcoin-miners/

https://www.reuters.com/business/sustainable-business/oil-drillers-bitcoin-miners-bond-over-natural-gas-2021-05-21/

https://www.crusoeenergy.com/blog

https://www.arabnews.com/node/1859426/business-economy

Figure 9: Bitcoin mining in an oil field.

Chapter 5: Review Questions

1. Which of the following best explains why NFTs have created new monetization opportunities for artists?

A. They allow artists to receive royalties on every resale of their work

B. NFTs remove the need for digital ownership verification

C. NFTs ensure that every piece of art remains unique and cannot be copied

D. Traditional galleries and music labels have adopted NFTs as their primary sales method

2. True or False? Meme coins, unlike ICOs, are legally required to have a clear utility and function within a project to be considered legitimate.

A. True

B. False

3. Which of the following statements about the metaverse is NOT true?

A. The metaverse consists of multiple virtual spaces, each with its own economy and digital assets

B. The metaverse is fully developed and widely used for all financial transactions

C. Blockchain technology enables digital ownership within the metaverse

D. The shift to virtual interactions has been accelerated by social trends and pandemic-related lockdowns

4. True or False? The high valuation of NFTs, such as digital collectibles like Bored Ape Yacht Club, is primarily driven by scarcity, social status, and digital exclusivity rather than traditional artistic merit.

A. True

B. False

5. Why is blockchain technology considered a financial revolution?

A. It allows for decentralized transactions without government intervention

B. It ensures that central banks can monitor and control digital assets more effectively

C. It provides a temporary solution until traditional banks integrate the system

D. It limits global financial participation by requiring high entry fees

6. True or False? One reason meme coins are compared to fashion trends is that their popularity is largely based on speculation, branding, and cultural relevance rather than inherent financial value.

A. True

B. False

7. Which of the following is NOT a characteristic of traditional banking?

A. Banks profit from lending deposits

B. Depositors earn high interest on savings

C. Banks require intermediaries for transactions

D. Banks often lend more money than they physically hold

8. True or False? Crossing an international border with more than $10,000 in cash or monetary instruments without declaration can result in fines or even imprisonment.

A. True

B. False

9. What is a key advantage of DeFi compared to traditional banking?

A. Higher transparency and profit-sharing for users

B. Lower interest rates for savers

C. Full reliance on physical cash reserves

D. Government-controlled financial transactions

10. True or False? Bitcoin's private keys are stored on a central server to ensure easy access if a user forgets their credentials.

A. True

B. False

11. How does Web 3 differ from Web 2?

A. Web 3 relies on centralized corporations for data control, while Web 2 does not

B. Web 3 integrates blockchain for decentralization and financial incentives, while Web 2 focuses on data monetization by corporations

C. Web 3 is entirely offline, while Web 2 is Internet-based

D. Web 3 eliminates digital interactions, whereas Web 2 encourages them

12. True or False? A seed phrase is a human-readable version of a private key that allows a user to recover their Bitcoin wallet if they lose access to their original device.

A. True

B. False

13. What is a key advantage of Bitcoin's portability compared to traditional forms of wealth?

A. Bitcoin transactions are completely anonymous with no record of ownership

B. Bitcoin wealth can be stored in one's memory using a seed phrase, making it easy to cross borders

C. Bitcoin is universally accepted as legal tender in all countries

D. Bitcoin does not require internet access to be transferred or used

14. True or False? If a user loses their private key or seed phrase, they can contact a third party for assistance in recovering their Bitcoin.

A. True

B. False

15. Which of the following statements about Bitcoin's private and public keys is true?

A. A public key allows users to access their Bitcoin holdings

B. A private key is used to send Bitcoin and should never be shared

C. Public keys and private keys function identically

D. Private keys are assigned by the government to prevent fraud

16. What is one major implication of Bitcoin for individuals without access to traditional banking?

A. It allows them to transact globally with only a phone and internet connection

B. It eliminates the need for any financial security precautions

C. It ensures all users will have the same level of wealth

D. It prevents inflation by regulating fiat currency exchange rates

Chapter 5: Answers

1. Which of the following best explains why NFTs have created new monetization opportunities for artists?

A. They allow artists to receive royalties on every resale of their work

B. NFTs remove the need for digital ownership verification

C. NFTs ensure that every piece of art remains unique and cannot be copied

D. Traditional galleries and music labels have adopted NFTs as their primary sales method

1. Answer: A. Smart contracts on a blockchain ensure that artists receive a percentage of resale profits, unlike traditional art markets.

2. True or False? Meme coins, unlike ICOs, are legally required to have a clear utility and function within a project to be considered legitimate.

A. True

B. False

2. Answer: B. False. Meme coins are purely speculative and legally cannot have any utility, making them highly volatile and unpredictable.)

3. Which of the following statements about the metaverse is NOT true?

A. The metaverse consists of multiple virtual spaces, each with its own economy and digital assets

B. The metaverse is fully developed and widely used for all financial transactions

C. Blockchain technology enables digital ownership within the metaverse

D. The shift to virtual interactions has been accelerated by social trends and pandemic-related lockdowns

3. Answer: B. The metaverse is still in development, and while virtual economies exist, it is not yet the primary space for all financial transactions.

4. True or False? The high valuation of NFTs, such as digital collectibles like Bored Ape Yacht Club, is primarily driven by scarcity, social status, and digital exclusivity rather than traditional artistic merit.

A. True

B. False

4. Answer: A. True. The appeal of NFTs often lies in exclusivity, brand association, and community access rather than traditional artistic valuation.

5. Why is blockchain technology considered a financial revolution?

A. It allows for decentralized transactions without government intervention

B. It ensures that central banks can monitor and control digital assets more effectively

C. It provides a temporary solution until traditional banks integrate the system

D. It limits global financial participation by requiring high entry fees

5. Answer: A. Blockchain decentralizes financial transactions, removing reliance on banks and intermediaries.

6. True or False? One reason meme coins are compared to fashion trends is that their popularity is largely based on speculation, branding, and cultural relevance rather than inherent financial value.

A. True

B. False

6. Answer: A. True. Like fashion brands, meme coins gain value through perception and community rather than utility.

7. Which of the following is NOT a characteristic of traditional banking?

A. Banks profit from lending deposits

B. Depositors earn high interest on savings

C. Banks require intermediaries for transactions

D. Banks often lend more money than they physically hold

7. Answer: B. Traditional banks offer low interest on deposits, while keeping most of the profits from lending activities.

8. True or False? Crossing an international border with more than $10,000 in cash or monetary instruments without declaration can result in fines or even imprisonment.

A. True

B. False

8. Answer: A. True. U.S. Customs enforces strict limits on undeclared monetary instruments; violating these limits can result in asset seizure and legal consequences.

9. What is a key advantage of DeFi compared to traditional banking?

A. Higher transparency and profit-sharing for users

B. Lower interest rates for savers

C. Full reliance on physical cash reserves

D. Government-controlled financial transactions

9. Answer: A. DeFi is more transparent and allows users to earn a greater share of financial gains.

10. True or False? Bitcoin's private keys are stored on a central server to ensure easy access if a user forgets their credentials.

A. True

B. False

10. Answer: B. False. Private keys are not stored centrally; they must be kept secure by the user, or access to the Bitcoin wallet is permanently lost.

11. How does Web 3 differ from Web 2?

A. Web 3 relies on centralized corporations for data control, while Web 2 does not

B. Web 3 integrates blockchain for decentralization and financial incentives, while Web 2 focuses on data monetization by corporations

C. Web 3 is entirely offline, while Web 2 is Internet-based

D. Web 3 eliminates digital interactions, whereas Web 2 encourages them

11. Answer: B. Web 3 decentralizes data storage and integrates financial incentives, contrasting with Web 2's corporate-driven model.

12. True or False? A seed phrase is a human-readable version of a private key that allows a user to recover their Bitcoin wallet if they lose access to their original device.

A. True

B. False

12. Answer: A. True. A seed phrase is a backup for a private key, enabling users to restore their wallets on new devices if necessary.

13. What is a key advantage of Bitcoin's portability compared to traditional forms of wealth?

A. Bitcoin transactions are completely anonymous with no record of ownership

B. Bitcoin wealth can be stored in one's memory using a seed phrase, making it easy to cross borders

C. Bitcoin is universally accepted as legal tender in all countries

D. Bitcoin does not require internet access to be transferred or used

13. Answer: B. A user can memorize a 12–24 word seed phrase, allowing them to retain access to their wealth without needing to physically carry assets.

14. True or False? If a user loses their private key or seed phrase, they can contact a third party for assistance in recovering their Bitcoin.

A. True

B. False

14. Answer: B. False. If a private key or seed phrase is lost, no third party can recover the Bitcoin; it is permanently inaccessible.

15. Which of the following statements about Bitcoin's private and public keys is true?

A. A public key allows users to access their Bitcoin holdings

B. A private key is used to send Bitcoin and should never be shared

C. Public keys and private keys function identically

D. Private keys are assigned by the government to prevent fraud

15. Answer: B. A private key allows a user to send Bitcoin and should be kept secret, as it provides full control over the associated funds.

16. What is one major implication of Bitcoin for individuals without access to traditional banking?

A. It allows them to transact globally with only a phone and internet connection

B. It eliminates the need for any financial security precautions

C. It ensures all users will have the same level of wealth

D. It prevents inflation by regulating fiat currency exchange rates

16. Answer: A. Bitcoin enables people without traditional bank accounts to conduct transactions globally using only a phone and internet access.

Chapter 6

Ethereum
by Eryka Gemma

Bitcoin is the most well-known of the cryptocurrencies, but there are also a number of new cryptocurrencies worth knowing about because they enable different types of opportunities for investors. This chapter will focus on Ethereum, a technology that was originally intended to be built on top of Bitcoin but instead utilized its own blockchain. Ethereum and the Ethereum Virtual Machine (EVM) has enabled tens of thousands of new cryptocurrencies to be built on top of its blockchain. Ethereum inspired BNB, XRP, Cardano, and Solana, and new cryptocurrencies are also being developed and issued from governments around the world.

The concept of cryptocurrencies based on the structure of blockchain technology is a fairly recent development, and smart investors will carefully examine the benefits and detriments of investing in these digital currency variations. Today, at the dawn of cryptocurrency investment, many investors are attracted to the idea of investing in what may someday become the Amazon, Apple or Microsoft of this new investment category. Choose carefully, for you may purchase into an investment that could set you up for life...or leave you empty-handed.

Objectives

In this chapter you will:

- Learn some interesting details about ethereum, the second largest blockchain by market cap.
- Recognize some differences between ethereum and bitcoin.
- Gain insight on what smart contracts do.
- Find out about the transaction speed differences between these two cryptocurrencies.
- Realize what makes ethereum a potentially good investment choice.

Though bitcoin is the most well-known of the cryptocurrencies, ethereum is also popular and may offer some advantages that bitcoin does not, which explains why these two currencies are competitive.

Ethereum

Ethereum and Bitcoin are both blockchain-based technologies, but while the Bitcoin blockchain permits only the sending and receiving of bitcoin, the Ethereum blockchain does the same and also allows a variety of additional decentralized applications (dApps) to build on top of its network through a protocol called "smart contracts", which are self-executing contracts based on predetermined code. Another advantage of the Ethereum technology is that it can process transactions much faster than Bitcoin.

The founders of Ethereum originally attempted to use bitcoin for smart contracts with a concept called colored coins. Due to scaling abilities and speed of the network, the founders of Ethereum created an entirely different blockchain.

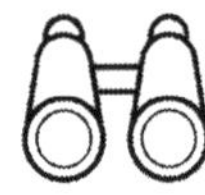

Definition:

Ether: The alternative cryptocurrency used on the Ethereum blockchain network.

The Ethereum network offers a digital currency called ether (ETH). Similar to bitcoin currency, ether can be mined by miners, and can be used to make payments for goods and services. Ether is the second biggest digital currency in the cryptocurrency market with a market capitalization in February 2025 of over $326 billion compared with bitcoin's $1940 billion market cap.

The biggest innovation of the Ethereum blockchain is the application of "smart contracts". A smart contract is a computer code that authorizes an activity when a previously determined condition is met. When the predefined conditions are met, it triggers actions such as releasing payments or executing other contract terms, all without the need for intermediaries. This allows the network's developers to create a smart contract for a variety of activities, such as fulfilling a service, storing data, distributing interest and balancing collateral levels.

An example would be a mortgage company processing paperwork on the sale of a house, and being paid with Ether upon the acceptance of the task's completion. Another example of a smart contract on the Ethereum network could be a dental office having a contract with its patients for 6-month cleanings, and upon seeing a patient for the prescribed appointment, a smart contract would authorize the payment of Ether to the dentist's office. These are examples of how the Ethereum blockchain can be employed in ways the Bitcoin network cannot.

Definition:

Smart contract: A computer procedure that digitally verifies an expected performance and authorizes payment based on the completion of the contract.

The entire decentralized finance industry would not be possible without Ethereum's Turing Complete Ethereum Virtual Machine (EVM). Turing complete means it has the ability to execute any computational task that a general-purpose computer can perform, provided there are sufficient resources. This is why Ethereum requires "gas fees", the compensation paid to miners and stakers for making transactions possible on the blockchains.

This capability gives Ethereum an advantage by enabling the development of sophisticated decentralized applications (DApps) and smart contracts. Unlike Bitcoin, which has a restricted scripting language, Ethereum's flexibility allows for more complex automation and a broader range of use cases on its blockchain.

Forks

Forks is a condition that affects both the Bitcoin and Ethereum networks, occurring when there is a change in the blockchain code, such as when a new protocol or feature is added to the blockchain. An example of this would be when there is a change to overcome network congestion or help operations become more efficient. Consensus is required before a fork can be accepted by the network so all the preceding blocks are validated.

One of the most well-known forks in Bitcoin's history occurred in 2017 when the network split into Bitcoin (BTC) and Bitcoin Cash (BCH). This was a highly debated and politically charged fork, with network participants divided over whether Bitcoin should adopt larger block sizes to handle more transactions.

The block size determines how much data each block on the blockchain can store. Supporters of Bitcoin Cash (BCH) argued that Bitcoin needed to scale beyond its 1 MB block size limit (later increased to 2 MB with SegWit) to accommodate higher transaction volumes. On the other hand, BTC supporters favored maintaining smaller blocks to preserve decentralization and keep full node operation accessible to more users.

The debate was fueled by lobbying, corporate interests, social media campaigns, and even propaganda, making it one of the most controversial moments in Bitcoin's history. Because a consensus was not reached, a hard fork took place, permanently splitting the network into two chains—BTC, which retained the smaller block size, and BCH, which increased the block size to 8 MB at launch.

If the majority of the Bitcoin network had agreed on larger blocks, a hard fork would not have been necessary and BTC could have scaled without creating a separate chain. However, the split reflected fundamental differences in philosophy with BTC prioritizing decentralization and security while BCH focused on increasing transaction throughput.

Ethereum's Advances

Use of the Ethereum blockchain increased dramatically in 2017 and the Ethereum network is expected to become quite popular. With its increasing market reach and the development of ever-increasing Ethereum applications, there are also several issues and challenges Ethereum needs to overcome.

The biggest challenge is increasing the number of confirmed transactions per second. Bitcoin can currently confirm about seven transactions per second, while Ethereum currently confirms about 20 transactions per second. At the moment, however, cryptotransactions are not yet a mass phenomenon, being conducted by only a slim minority of Internet users, but when this situation changes and the number of users grows exponentially as is expected, the network capable of making more rapid transactions will be preferred.

Key:
Bitcoin can only complete about seven transactions per second compared with Ethereum's around 20 transactions per second.

As the pervasiveness of blockchain technology and blockchain network transactions become mainstream, the system will need to handle thousands of transactions per second. To be prepared for this, the Ethereum Developer Team has created a technology called Casper. According to Ethereum founder Vitalik Buterin, Casper technology was able to confirm up to 20,000 transactions per second in 2023.

Ethereum's Pending Uses

It is expected that the Ethereum network will revolutionize the health-care system. The Ethereum blockchain system will allow all hospitals around the world to store, access and share patients' records. This level of data sharing can become a key factor with developing new vaccines to overcome viral outbreaks, or even prevent them from ever taking hold in a population. When you are traveling in Ecuador and visit a doctor for a check-up with a visit later with your doctor in Chicago when you return home, both facilities will have access to the same medical information about you.

Definition:

Server farm. A server farm is a facility dedicated to housing hundreds of servers that process and store digital information.

Dropbox and Microsoft warehouse huge amounts of data in big server farms. One of the concerns about server farms is that the company concentrates a lot of its storage capacity in a single location and the company can suffer substantial losses if the building or buildings are destroyed by a natural disaster or terrorist attack.

The solution to this potential disaster is a decentralized storage facility where information is not stored in a few large server farms in the U.S., but in hundreds or thousands of data centers all around the world. Until recently this has not been realistic because it's a technological challenge to build a network connecting hundreds of servers safely while ensuring fast data-transfer. However, Ethereum is very likely to be the first to develop a solution to this problem because its blockchain technology is highly virile and can quickly encrypt and transfer data between millions of servers.

Note:
Ethereum may be first to solve the issue of creating faster transactions between servers.

The gambling industry in the U.S. is estimated to be worth about $250 trillion, and is a true black market. As the Internet became mainstream in the late '90s, the first online casinos and sports books began to appear. While it's likely that "real-world" casinos and sports betting books lack transparency, imagine the extent of activity being conducted on dark online gambling websites! One of the core features of Ethereum technology is that its rapid, accurate, and private transactions can completely disrupt the online casino industry...as well as have the effect of promoting online gambling since players will no longer need to fear scams and fraud, or criminal influences.

You may have heard of Polymarket, a decentralized prediction market built on Ethereum allowing users to bet on real-world events such as elections, financial trends, and cultural happenings. Unlike traditional betting platforms, it operates globally without intermediaries, using blockchain technology to ensure transparency and security. By leveraging smart contracts, Polymarket automates wagers and payouts, preventing manipulation and eliminating the need for centralized oversight.

Its innovative model treats bets as tradable assets, meaning users can buy and sell positions before an event concludes, creating a dynamic and liquid marketplace. The platform's ability to aggregate collective intelligence has made it a powerful forecasting tool, often outperforming traditional polls. However, its rapid growth and lack of formal regulation have drawn scrutiny from authorities, leading to legal challenges, such as the FBI's 2024 investigation into its CEO. It can be speculated that the seizing of the CEO's phone was politically driven, especially since Polymarket's users predominantly bet on Donald Trump's victory in the presidential election, contradicting mainstream polls. This perspective is reinforced by Polymarket CEO Shayne Coplan, who described the investigation as "obvious political retribution".

Despite regulatory uncertainty, Polymarket remains a groundbreaking platform that blends finance, technology, and market-driven predictions in a way that traditional betting sites cannot replicate.

ERC-20 Tokens

ERC are the initials for Ethereum Request for Comments which is the process used for recommending improvements to the Ethereum network. The number 20 happens to be the proposal identification number or token standard used to define a common set of rules for fungible tokens on the Ethereum network.

ERC-20 tokens represent an asset a user can employ in a variety of ways. They are tradeable like coins, loyalty points or currencies. They are fungible and can be redeemed for goods or services if acceptable by the recipient. Obviously, ERC-20 tokens are used on the Ethereum blockchain network and can be used on any platforms, wallets, and decentralized applications (dApps) that Ethereum utilizes. Fundamentally, ERC-20 tokens are smart contracts that automate and enforce predefined rules for transactions and token interactions. compliant. These tokens are essentially smart contracts used to compensate a user for designated task completions or represent data in a specific industry.

Chapter 6: Review Questions

1. Two advantages of Ethereum over Bitcoin are:

    A. The Ethereum blockchain allows more applications to be handled than the Bitcoin block chain does

    B. Ethereum can process transactions faster than Bitcoin

    C. Ethereum transaction fees are more than Litecoin's

    D. Choices A and B

    E. Choices A and C

    F. Choices B and C

2. Ether is the second biggest cryptocurrency available today as measured by market cap. True or false?

    A. True.

    B. False.

3. A smart contract is:

    A. A transaction only done by a cell phone

    B. A prearranged payment for a performed task

    C. A contract between two attorneys

    D. A transaction between Bitcoin and Ethereum

4. What is a fork?

   A. A market split between Bitcoin, Litecoin, and Ether.

   B. A change in the intention of a smart contract

   C. A change in the blockchain code

   D. A change in the speed of transaction completions

Chapter 6: Answers

1. Two advantages of Ethereum over Bitcoin are:

   A. The Ethereum blockchain allows more applications to be handled than the Bitcoin block chain does

   B. Ethereum can process transactions faster than Bitcoin

   C. Ethereum transaction fees are more than Litecoin's

   D. Choices A and B

   E. Choices A and C

   F. Choices B and C

   Answer: D. Choices A and B are correct. Choice C is a red herring as the question is about Bitcoin and Ethereum, not Litecoin.

2. Ether is the second biggest cryptocurrency available today as measured by market cap. True or false?

   A. True.

   B. False.

   Answer: A. True. Ether's market capitalization was $320 billion as of Feb 2025, compared with Bitcoin's $1940 billion.

3. A smart contract is:

   A. A transaction only done by a cell phone

   B. A prearranged payment for a performed task

   C. A contract between two attorneys

D. A transaction between Bitcoin and Ethereum

Answer: B. A smart contract pre-arranges the payment of a perform task upon completion.

4. What is a fork?

A. A market split between Bitcoin, Litecoin, and Ether.

B. A change in the intention of a smart contract

C. A change in the blockchain code

D. A change in the speed of transaction completions

Answer: C. There are times when the blockchain code is adjusted to remedy a situation. Upon consensus, the fork is authenticated.

Chapter 7

Emerging Cryptocurrencies, AKA Altcoins, and Wallets

We've looked at only a few cryptocurrencies ... bitcoin and ethereum ... and in mid-2023 there were about 25,000 different active cryptocurrencies around the planet, and more seem to be added every week. With so many cryptocurrencies available worldwide, investigating these potential investments and deciding whether or not to include them in your alternative portfolio can be a rather daunting task.

This chapter will give you a brief overview of alternative cryptocurrencies, and a beginner's insight on how to hold and trade them, providing exposure that may be the starting point for educating yourself about making informed decisions on the underlying value of encrypted currencies.

Objectives

In this chapter you will:

- Learn more about altcoins and how they may or may not be better than Bitcoin.
- Find out if privacy coins are truly private.
- Understand the risks of investing in an ICO.
- Have a clear idea about how to purchase cryptocurrencies.

- Identify your choices about where to store your cryptocurrency.
- Acquire a more complete understanding about the five different types of digital wallets.
- Discover the difference between hot and cold storage.
- Know the safest place to store your cryptocurrency wealth.

The word "altcoins" refers to any alternative cryptocurrency that appeared after Bitcoin was established as a reliably tradeable currency. Altcoins represent themselves as improved substitutes to Bitcoin, although this is not necessarily true and definitely subject to close scrutiny.

Definition:

Altcoin: An altcoin is any alternative cryptocurrency that appeared after bitcoin was established as a reliably tradeable currency.

One of the strategies founders of new altcoins employ is to identify limitations of Bitcoin and then create improved versions that represent desired advantages. Many altcoins are quite similar to Bitcoin, being peer-to-peer, employing a mining process, and providing a means for conducting secure and private transactions on the web. Yet, there are some significant differences such as using different economic models or varied coin-distribution methods.

Other altcoins use alternative proof-of-work mining algorithms, or don't require any proof-of -work at all. There are some altcoins that provide a more universal programming language that allow other programmers to build additional applications, while others provide additional privacy in excess of what Bitcoin provides.

In contrast to these innovations, there are also a lot of altcoins that don't offer any worthy variations at all. They might make some minor improvements that don't matter much or offer something that sounds useful but really has no value. An example would be an altcoin that offers a greater number of coins, but which really only limits the value of each coin because the total amount of coins is so vast.

Note:
Though many altcoins are being created, most of them offer very little or no benefit over bitcoin.

Many altcoins offer no benefit over Bitcoin at all, and may be deficient with their hash security or have other decisively impairing quirks such as networks that are too small, too few developers working on improvements, possessing more risk than Bitcoin, having more volatile exchange rates, etc. The fact is that thus far, over the years Bitcoin still stands above most of the newer issues as many of its competitors have come and gone. Indeed, not just a few proved to be scams to seduce the gullible, benefiting only the inventors and a few of the early adopters.

Privacy Coins

Because of the pervasiveness of technology in our lives and the numerous ways our identities can be compromised, the concept of privacy coins is very appealing to people who wish to conduct their transactions without being identified. While Bitcoin transactions are partly anonymous, they are not completely so. This is because the transactions on the blockchain are publicly visible so every node can choose to give or withhold consensus, however, while the wallet is identified through its public address, the identity of the owner of the wallet remains private.

This is only a superficial privacy because eventually most users will choose to cash out some or all of their wealth, which means being observed when the transferred cash appears in their bank accounts. Privacy coins use a disseminated public ledger but employ a different technology that camouflages transactions. The amount of the transaction is not disguised, but the trail from sender to recipient is not revealed.

Key:
Privacy coins are not always private.

Zcash is a privacy coin that uses a public blockchain and offers users the opportunity to conceal the sender, recipient, and amount of the transaction, or choose the option to be transparent. The level of privacy is sufficient for most people and as it turns out, presently only a small number of its users choose the privacy features. For those individuals who require a deeper level of privacy, Monero is the cryptocurrency of choice. Its technology is highly regarded and used by deep web marketplaces where the need for strongly concealed financial transactions is critical.

Even though the moniker of privacy coin suggests a cloak of invisibility for the user and his or her transactions, almost anything on the web can be compromised and if the three-letter agencies choose to hack into your account to identify you and your business, there is very little you can do about it unless you have the resources of someone like Dr. No. Most people will be satisfied with the level of concealment offered by privacy coins, or they should not be conducting their business online.

ICOs

An ICO is an Initial Coin Offering and is used by founders of a cryptocurrency in much the same way that IPOs (Initial Public Offerings) are used to raise funds to capitalize a company so the managers can develop essential components needed to secure the company's presence in the marketplace. ICOs have been used since 2013 to fund cryptocurrencies. Founders and managers of a new cryptocurrency will authorize the creation of a pre-created token that can then be sold on exchanges to acquire the capital needed to hire talent or invest in infrastructure.

As there are many people interested in investing in the "next Bitcoin" before it becomes big and increases exponentially in value, many ICOs may exist only on paper as a concept waiting for funding which may or may never materialize. Investment fraud is always a concern and the wise investor will look into the formation of ICOs with caution because of the high risk involved.

Presently the legal state of ICOs is benignly regulated and mostly undefined, which of course increases risks for investors while also creating a range of opportunities. ICOs are often referred to as "crowd sales" because regulatory authority is usually unavailable.

Note:
Buyer beware, because ICOs can be fraudulent since government regulation at this time is inconsistent.

Some jurisdictions are now becoming aware of ICOs and are choosing to regulate them in the same way as the sale of shares in securities.

As always, the smart investor researches investment opportunities to more clearly understand the nature of the investment, its benefits and risks. When investing in ICOs, special attention should be paid to the members of the development team and advisory board. As you research their backgrounds, look for relevant experience and try to determine the degree of success each member has already enjoyed in developing and marketing cryptocurrencies. Also determine the value and significance of the company's underlying concept, find out if there is a beta version being tested, and if there is any evidence of a prototype product available for your assessment.

Digital Wallets for Cryptocurrencies

As you know from before, cryptocurrency is transmitted between digital wallets, from one address on the ledger to another. Most cryptocurrencies have their own official wallet, but may recommend wallets available through third parties. If you wish to trade and hold cryptocurrencies, you will need some form of a cryptocurrency wallet. Your wallet contains your private and public keys, allowing you to send and receive cryptocoins, and acts as your personal ledger, keeping track of all your transactions.

Key:
The safest digital wallet is the hardware wallet or paper wallet because your cryptocurrency wealth is not always online.

Security is a key factor of digital wallets, obviously, and the degree of security is different from wallet to wallet. A good practice is not to keep more currency than necessary in a wallet you use frequently, just as you would not walk down a dark street with a wallet stuffed with $100 bills. There are many ways to increase your wallet's security, such as by using Authy or Google Authenticator to increase your layers of protection, encrypting your digital wallet, and using an official or officially endorsed wallet. You could also employ multi-signature transactions, encrypt your wallet and private keys, and keep backup copies on a CD or thumb drive in case you need to reference this data. Should you lose your wallet or your keys, you will also lose the currency they protect.

5 Different Types of Cryptocurrency Wallets

Here are some of the more popular wallets being used today:

1. Desktop Wallet: A desktop wallet is the most common type of digital currency wallet, usually consisting of an application located on a user's computer screen.

2. Online Wallet: An online wallet is web-based. An app is not downloaded to a user's computer, but instead the user accesses the wallet through a website's server.

3. Mobile Wallet: A mobile wallet is a wallet connected through an app on a smart phone.

4. Hardware Wallet: This level of wallet is dedicated hardware built specifically to contain cryptocurrency and hold it securely. A hardware wallet can access online transactions to retrieve data and can then go off-line and be transported for convenience and security.

5. Paper Wallet: If you wish to avoid keeping digital data about your currency online, you can use a paper wallet. This would require printing a QR code for your public and private keys, allowing you to send and receive digital currency without having to store your currency information online.

Hot and Cold Storage

Hot Storage: Hot storage is when a user keeps his or her cryptocurrency in a device that's directly connected to the Internet. Because it's constantly connected, it is easy to access funds in a hot wallet, and if there are shops where you live that accept cryptocoins for micropayments, it could be very convenient using hot storage for day-to-day spending. It would be very much the same as carrying around fiat (government issued) currency as you are already used to doing. Of course, you would only want to keep a portion of your cryptowealth in a wallet for convenience with the majority secured elsewhere.

Your hot wallet would serve you in the same way as a real-world paper bill wallet. There is, however, a large drawback to using a hot storage wallet and that is that they are easily hackable.

Key:
The safest digital wallet is the hardware wallet because your cryptocurrency wealth is not always online.

As cryptocurrencies become more prevalent, crime is never far behind. Recent ransomware attacks and the security breaches of large exchanges should be sufficient beacons to warn newcomers wanting to protect the value in their pockets.

Cold Storage: Cold storage is storing your currency in a device that is completely off-line, like a hardware wallet. This provides the most secure form of storage and is a good choice for owners of cryptocurrency who want to store their wealth over the long-term, and don't need access to their cryptocoins for months, or even years. Because of the ever present risk of determined hackers, cold storage minimizes the risk of theft and is the most secure option for safely storing your money.

Note:
"Hacking has been a repeating issue for this industry from the earliest starting point. Indeed, a report a year ago from the US Department of Homeland Security found that 33% of Bitcoin trades were hacked in the vicinity of 2009 and 2015, and one-off tricks and assaults on singular financial specialists have been happening all through that time also." (Source: Steemit.com, January, 2018.)

Storage Security: Some investors store their cryptocoins on cryptocurrency exchanges, and while this is a relatively secure practice, it is not advised over the long-term or for a large amount of cryptocoins. The reason is that exchanges are frequently targets of criminal hackers who are, unfortunately, always devising new methods to break the security of these exchanges and steal cryptocoin wealth. Many exchanges have been victimized by hacking theft, so it is advised that investors keep a minimal amount of their cryptowealth in the exchange for use but remove any excesses for safer keeping in a more secure digital wallet.

Summary

In these early days there seems to be no end to the development of new cryptocurrencies around the globe, and as this new asset class develops a history of performance and a track record of security, the concept of owning, trading, and investing in cryptocurrencies will become more common.

Eventually, of course, the Model T Fords and Edsels will get weeded out and standards will be set. Once the flurry of new cryptocurrencies has peaked and then settled, there will be a few nationally and globally accepted cryptocurrencies that will become as commonplace as the dollar or the yen. Investors and users will become familiar with the varieties of wallets and their uses, and the daily exchange of currency for value will continue as it has for thousands of years, except now it will be based on a 21st century belief in the implied worth of ephemeral digital evidence.

Chapter 7: Review Questions

1. In mid-2023, about how many different active cryptocurrencies were there around the world?

    A. 250

    B. 2,500

    C. 25,000

    D. 250,000

2. Altcoins are alternative currency:

    A. To cryptocurrencies such as gold or fiat currency

    B. To metal coins, paper money, or tokens

    C. That are clearly superior to Bitcoin

    D. That represent themselves as improved substitutes to Bitcoin but may not be so

3. Which of the following choices is not true about altcoins?

    A. They always offer benefits over Bitcoin

    B. They employ a mining process

    C. They provide secure transactions

    D. They are peer-to-peer

4. Privacy coins are completely private. True or false?

    A. True

    B. False

5. Initial Coin Offerings (ICOs):

    A. Are used to raise funds to capitalize a company

    B. Could be fraudulent

C. May use pre-created tokens

D. Appeal to investors looking for the "next Bitcoin"

E. Are always regulated by the government

F. Are partly regulated by the government

Which of these statements is not true?

6. A cryptocurrency wallet:

A. Contains a public key

B. Contains a private key

C. Acts as a personal ledger

D. Allows the owner to send and receive cryptocoins

E. Provides completely guaranteed security

F. Encrypts transactions

Which of the preceding is not true?

7. It's always a good idea to keep a backup copy of your cryptocurrency wallet on a CD or thumb drive. True or false?

A. True

B. False

8. This type of wallet is considered the safest:

A. Desktop wallet

B. Online wallet

C. Mobile wallet

D. Hardware wallet

E. Paper wallet

9. You should periodically remove excess wealth from your hot storage wallet. True or false?

A. True

B. False

10. This type of cryptocurrency storage serves the user in the same way as a real -world paper bill wallet.

A. Hot storage

B. Cold storage

Chapter 7: Answers

1. How many different active cryptocurrencies are there today, around the world?

   A. 220

   B. 2,200

   C. 22,000

   D. 220,000

   Answer: C. There are presently 25,000 different cryptocurrencies, and more are regularly being created.

2. Altcoins are alternative currency:

   A. To cryptocurrencies such as gold or fiat currency

   B. To metal coins, paper money, or tokens

   C. That are clearly superior to Bitcoin

   D. That represent themselves as improved substitutes to Bitcoin but may not be so

   Answer: D. Some altcoins have benefits that exceed the advantages of Bitcoin, but most altcoins do not.

3. Which of the following choices is not true about altcoins?

   A. They always offer benefits over Bitcoin

   B. They employ a mining process

   C. They provide secure transactions

   D. They are peer-to-peer

   Answer: A. Not all altcoins are superior to Bitcoin.

4. Privacy coins are completely private. True or false?

    A. True

    B. False

    Answer: B. False. Privacy coins offer some degree of privacy, but are not completely private.

5. Initial Coin Offerings (ICOs):

    A. Are used to raise funds to capitalize a company

    B. Could be fraudulent

    C. May use pre-created tokens

    D. Appeal to investors looking for the "next Bitcoin"

    E. Are always regulated by the government

    F. Are partly regulated by the government

    Which of these statements is not true?

    Answer: F. Presently, the Securities and Exchange Commission, the Chicago Mercantile Exchange, Commodity Futures Trading Commission, and the Financial Industry Regulatory Authority are all involved in some regard.

6. A cryptocurrency wallet:

    A. Contains a public key

    B. Contains a private key

    C. Acts as a personal ledger

    D. Allows the owner to send and receive cryptocoins

    E. Provides completely guaranteed security

    F. Encrypts transactions

Which of the preceding is not true?

Answer: E. Unfortunately, there is no wallet yet that can provide completely guaranteed security. Cold storage in a hardware while it appears to be the best choice at this time.

7. It's always a good idea to keep a backup copy of your cryptocurrency wallet on a CD or thumb drive. True or false?

A. True

B. False

Answer: A. True. When it comes to protecting your wealth, having a backup copy of your cryptocurrency wallet and related information is always a great idea.

8. This type of wallet is considered the safest:

A. Desktop wallet

B. Online wallet

C. Mobile wallet

D. Hardware wallet

E. Paper wallet

Answer: D. The reason the hardware wallet is the safest is because it is not always online where can be hacked.

9. You should periodically remove excess wealth from your hot storage wallet. True or false?

A. True

B. False

Answer: A. True. Because digital wallets can be hacked, it's always a good idea to store the bulk of your cryptocurrency wealth in a more secure wallet. Cold storage in a hardware wallet appears to be the best choice at this time.

10. This type of cryptocurrency storage serves the user in the same way as a real -world paper bill wallet.

A. Hot storage

B. Cold storage

Answer: A. Hot storage is kept in a wallet that is available for use on a regular basis, much like a paper bill wallet in your pocket.

Chapter 8

Government Involvement

One of the key benefits of cryptocurrency and blockchain technology is their independence from third-party control with the dissemination of processing and consensus reliably foisted onto the users of the network rather than, as has been the case until now, the cumbersome control of a centralized, costly, bureaucratic authority.

However, there may be some advantages to the imposition of governmental oversight given the continuing potential for ongoing fraud and criminal activity that has conspicuously infiltrated the realm of cryptocurrency, and which could substantially defend honest users and legitimate transactions while also curtailing fraud, drug trafficking, felonious activities, and terrorist funding.

Objectives

In this chapter you will:

- Understand why government regulation of cryptocurrencies is important.
- Identify the greatest concerns of international governments about the advent of cryptocurrencies.
- Know about two possible implementations the

U.S. government could take to establish a national cryptocurrency in the United States.

- Become familiar with the purpose of the SEC's Cyber Unit.
- Learn about the Silk Road and why this example alarms law enforcement agencies.
- Find out about the two reasons why the U.S. government favors a national cryptocurrency.

A Government Currency?

A number of national governments are testing the concept of authorizing and deploying cryptocurrency in their economy, among them Great Britain, China, Russia, and India. The United States has also expressed interest in exploring the idea and is developing a bank-to-bank digital currency, two other possible implementations are being discussed, government action appears to be distant.

The first potential application would be disbursing funds through accounts which are directly linked to the Federal Reserve. The National Bureau For Economic Research (NBER) conducted a review and determined this approach would "foster true price stability" because monetary policy would then be implemented among consumers.

A second option would be having the Federal Reserve partner with private banks to implement the spread of cryptocurrency use, which is similar to the way fiat funds are currently disbursed. The U.S. government is moving, albeit slowly, in this direction, considering ways to officially integrate cryptocurrency into our national economy.

"It's premature to be talking about the Federal Reserve offering digital currencies, but it is something we are starting to think about," said William Dudley, president of the Federal Reserve Bank of New York in November 2017.[3]

There are two main reasons why our government would be interested in legitimizing cryptocurrency. The first reason is to limit the amount of illegal activity being conducted with cryptocurrency as a form of cash. One of the key benefits of cash is that it is anonymous. Whether you put cash in your vault or under your mattress, no one can trace your use of it. With a national cryptocurrency, criminals would find it much harder to hoard money or use it for illicit purposes because every transaction would be registered in the government ledger and if a transaction was illegal, the users would be identified and held accountable.

The other reason our government would support a national cryptocurrency is because it could help strengthen monetary policy and assist with managing the economy.

Note:
The U.S. government is beginning to think about offering a digital currency not only to control criminal activities and strengthen monetary policy, but also to keep U.S. currency modern and maintain parity with other nations adopting a national digital currency.

As we are seeing with so many other elements of our society, the digital revolution is changing the way we think about

[3] Wall Street Journal, November 29, 2017.

money and we appear to be moving forward toward a cashless society, which was predicted decades ago by futurists. With modern technology now capable of instituting such a massive change in our spending, saving, and investing activities, it appears to be only a matter of time until we regard paper money and metal coins with nostalgia, fading from our daily view much like milk bottles, floppy disks and typewriters.

Examples of Government Cryptocurrency Regulation in Asia

In September 2017, the Japanese government recognized 11 cryptocurrency exchanges with the caveat they meet cybersecurity standards that would prevent money laundering. Today, in 2023, there are 32 exchanges.

The people of China have been very active in Bitcoin trading, and prior to 2017 they accounted for about 90% of all global Bitcoin trading. Since then, the Chinese government has forbidden Initial Coin Offerings and also closed several popular cryptocurrency exchanges. The effect of this crackdown caused the price of Bitcoins to plummet more than 40% in September 2017. Concerned about risks in the market, Vice Governor Pan Gongsheng of the People's Bank of China stated that the government would continue its pressure on digital currency and exhorted national and local authorities to ban exchanges that permitted the trading of Bitcoins and other virtual currencies. Also targeted were online wallet service providers. However, in 2023 there are several new policy changes that indicate a softening attitude toward cryptocurrencies in China. Though not the same as a cryptocurrency, there is a digital yuan.

U.S. Government Regulatory Agencies

In September 2017,the United States' Security Exchange Commission (SEC) established a new Cyber Unit whose purpose is to target cyber-related misconduct such as market manipulation schemes, hacking, violations of ledger technology, misconduct on the dark web, intrusions into retail brokerage accounts, and cyber-related threats. "Cyber-related threats and misconduct are among the greatest risks facing investors and the securities industry," said Stephanie Avakian, Co-Director of the SEC's Enforcement Division. "The Cyber Unit will enhance our ability to detect and investigate cyberthreats through increasing expertise in an area of critical national importance."[4]

Note:
The SEC has established a Cyber Unit to target cyber-related threats.

Soon after, the Cyber Unit filed its first complaint, establishing its serious intent to regulate cryptocurrency activities. The complaint was against the cryptocurrency firm PlexCorps, alleging that the company had defrauded its customers and failed to follow rules for offering U.S. securities. To this date, the SEC has not yet approved any exchange-traded products which hold cryptocurrencies or assets related to cryptocurrencies for listing or trading, nor has it accepted the registration of any Initial Coin Offerings. As of late March

[4] United States Securities and Exchange Commission, Press Release #2017-176, September 25, 2017.

2018, the SEC website contains warnings of potential risk and fraud to investors who may be interested in ICOs.

Key:
Cryptocurrency products traded on exchanges have not yet been approved by the SEC.

Another government agency, the Commodity Futures Trading Commission (CFTC), declared its authority over Bitcoin as authorized by interstate commerce commodity futures regulations to protect consumers from fraud and manipulation. CFTC Chair Christopher Giancarlo stated in 2018 that cryptocurrencies are not a fad and must be regulated by the government to protect investors and nurture the fledgling industry.

"Virtual currencies mark a paradigm shift in how we think about payments, traditional financial processes, and engaging in economic activity. Ignoring these developments will not make them go away, nor is it a responsible regulatory response. The evolution of these assets, their volatility, and the interest they attract from a rising global millennial population demand serious examination."[5]

The Internal Revenue Service (IRS) has also declared its interest by ruling that bitcoin and other cryptocurrencies are going to be regarded as property for tax purposes, and not

[5] Written Testimony of Chairman J. Christopher Giancarlo before the Senate Banking Committee, Washington, D.C., February 6, 2018.

as currencies. Stating that some exchanges may correctly issue Form 1099 for the acquisition of miscellaneous income, individuals are responsible for keeping track of their gains and paying tax. Transactions in cryptocurrencies which result in short-term or long-term capital gains or losses must be filed with the IRS.

Key:

The IRS has ruled that cryptocurrencies are property, not currencies, and gains or losses must be filed with the IRS.

International Regulation

Cryptocurrencies also pose issues for the international banking and economic community and the International Monetary Fund's (IMF) Managing Director, Christine Lagarde, stated that the IMF is actively working with national governments to prevent the use of digital currencies for money laundering or financing terrorism.

Definition:

Fintech: Technology that supports thanking and financial services.

In addition, at the recent 2018 World Economic Forum held in Davos, Switzerland this past January, U.S. Treasury Secretary Steven Mnuchin stated U.S. interest in developing more regulation to control the development and use of cryptocurrencies. "We encourage fintech, we encourage innovation, but we want to make sure that all of our financial markets are safe and aren't being used for illicit activities."[6]

Also evidencing concern about the use of cryptocurrencies and the need for government regulation, British Prime Minister Theresa May stated that the British government would "very seriously" regard cryptocurrencies "because of the way they are used, particularly by criminals."[7]

Clearly, national governments and the international community have realistic concerns about cryptocurrencies as a form of payment used in exchange for illegal activities and the worldwide threat of terrorism.

Privacy and Transparency

Aside from the criminal use of cryptocurrencies, and aside from the revolutionary aspect of blockchain technology as a system liberated from third-party control, the most important aspect to users who engage in cryptocurrency transactions is the concern over the privacy or transparency of their transactions, and the security of their wealth.

Blockchain's decentralized public ledger records every transaction and offers users both privacy and transparency. While every transaction is published and linked to a public key representing a unique user, the key is encrypted so it's not possible to identify an individual or corporate entity. Individuals and corporate entities are known only by their public key, and it is possible that this exposure could identify the user, much like an IP address identifies a point of origination.

---

[6] CNN, January 26, 2018.

[7] CNN, February 11, 2018.

While many users may have no concern about being identified, there are probably an equal number of individuals and entities that would prefer anonymity. Presently, privacy can be maintained except, as pointed out, not when there are determined hackers or three-letter government agencies relentlessly seeking access to your account.

Note:

Cryptocurrency exchanges have been successfully attacked. Here are some examples:

- 2025: ByBit hacked for $1.5 billion of Ethereum
- 2019: Binance hacked for $40 million; Upbit hacked for $45 million
- 2019: 2017: Tether hacked for $31 million
- 2016: Bitfinex hacked for $77 million; the DAO hacked for $50 million
- 2014: Mt. Gox hacked for $450 million
- 2012: Linode hacked for $200,000; Bitfloor hacked for $250,000

Source: Steemit.com, January, 2018; Crystalblockchain.com, June 2021. New York Times, 2025.

Security

When it comes to wealth and data protection, personal and business users require guaranteed security with transactions that are quick, inexpensive and stress-free. Blockchain technology could be a panacea for the entire online security industry, capable of addressing global security issues with data that travels across international boundaries with unquestioned legitimacy.

Network decentralization that authenticates data transactions through consensus is effective in verifying the integrity of the transmissions and limits the likelihood of a successful attack by cyber criminals, though we are still in the early years of this digital revolution and the lapse in security that allowed the huge losses for the exchanges identified above must give users pause and inspire them to act wisely by employing cold storage for the largest portion of their holdings.

Cryptocurrencies and Black Markets

Regulation creates black markets. Imposing restrictions that limit legal access to certain goods, services, or financial systems – driving demand underground. Black markets are often seen as places for drug activity to thrive but they are also backlashes to costly compliance and restrictive pricing. These markets create transactions which occur outside government oversight, often fostering increased risk, lack of consumer protections, and even criminal activity. Cryptocurrencies, like cash or any any item of value, can attract the attention and darkly clever misuse of criminal influences.

The example of a research scientist named Ross Ulbricht should provide shocking insight into one of the first widely adopted use cases made possible through the cryptocurrency networks. In late 2010 when Bitcoin was still relatively unknown and Ulbricht was a recent graduate from Pennsylvania State University, he became interested in becoming an entrepreneur and began his own video game company. On his LinkedIn page, Ulbricht stated he was "creating an economic simulation to give people a first-hand experience of what it would be like to live in a world without the systemic use of force. Ulbricht believed that people should have the right to buy and sell whatever they wanted, so long as they weren't hurting anyone else. This aligns with the libertarian non-aggression principle.

Attracted by the allure of free markets, Ulbricht launched an internet service called The Silk Road in February 2011. This site became a nexus for the sale of items driven into a black market due to strict regulations. The silk road items were 70+% marijuana sales but you could also find things like Accutane, an acne medicine made extremely expensive by big pharma, books, and art. Human trafficking was banned from the site but otherwise, it was a true agora. Naturally, drugs and illegal substances were sold on the site and only bitcoins was allowed for transactions. Narcotics orders could be made anonymously from the convenience of an individual's personal computer with delivery through the mail. This took drugs off the street corners, reducing violence and providing clarity as sellers and buyers were rated in an eBay like atmosphere. The Silk Road became popular very quickly because of its mail order service, which helped popularize Bitcoin among individuals who might not otherwise have been interested.

Ulbricht, operating under the pseudonym Dread Pirate Roberts, or DPR, eventually was found by law enforcement which seized his operation and put him into a federal penitentiary with a double life sentence plus 40 years without possibility for parole. His case was highly politicized with major interference from the press claiming he was involved in activities that were later dismissed by the judge with prejudice. Ross Ulbricht was ultimately charged with and convicted of seven counts related to his operation of the Silk Road website: Narcotics trafficking conspiracy, Distribution of narcotics by means of the internet, Continuing criminal enterprise, Computer hacking conspiracy, Money laundering conspiracy, Conspiracy to traffic fraudulent identity document and conspiracy to commit computer hacking. You'll note that nearly all of the charges include "conspiracy to" inferring that he did not actually commit those crimes but was found guilty of agreeing to and participating in plans to eventually commit those crimes.

Ulbricht's punishment was cruel and unusual. It was stated by the prosecutor that Ulbricht's libertarian ideologies and his implementation of them through Silk Road posed a significant threat to society and the rule of law, warranting severe punishment. His sentence was intended to set a precedent as a warning to others who might be interested in dark net activities. However, in practice this was not the case. The FBI agents who actually used the site to sell drugs were given less than 10 years.

Today, drugs are being actively sold on Facebook, snapchat and Twitter but prosecutors have not called Zuckerberg into a courtroom for drug trafficking. Ross made a website that used bitcoin, he didn't tell people what to sell on the site but it was made clear by the prosecution that his ideology was what was dangerous. In January of 2025, President Donald Trump awarded Ross with a full pardon citing that the same district (southern district of new York) also wrongfully went after Trump. This was a huge win as it can be argued that Ross maybe did deserve time in prison but his victimless crime did not deserve a double life +40 year sentence for a 30 year old, first time offender.

Many owe Ross a thank you exposing them to Bitcoin's capabilities when the price was $0.30.

Of course, criminals are always willing to take risks and since the Silk Road was shut down, a number of black markets have appeared and are still in use.

Summary

It's curious to think the excitement of cryptocurrency's initial *raison d'être* was the freedom from third-party control that inspired the techno-visionaries, and yet, because of the vagaries of the human character, some degree of third-party control is a necessity. Criminal behavior is just as prevalent with digital currencies as it has always been with fiat currencies, so some form of government regulation will eventually become mandatory, both to stem the profligacy of unmonitored greed as well as to render unto Caesar what is Caesar's in the form of digitally acquired capital gains taxes.

It is only a matter of time until the U.S. government adopts a national cryptocurrency and we take another step forward into the future that was prophesied in the 1950s, and perhaps earlier. Almost all major authorities concur that the sun is rising on cryptocurrency's day, and the only question that remains now is when national governments will establish national currencies, the nature of the government regulations that will be imposed, the content of the educational programs necessary to instruct the populace on their usability, and, perhaps, the modification of ATM machines around the world to accept the values held by cryptocurrency credit and debit cards.

Privacy, transparency, and security will likely always be issues with which the public and governments will have to contend as these three issues lie at the core of human behavior and our emotionally intimate relationship with money.

Chapter 8: Review Questions

1. Which of these choices is one of the two possible implementations the United States government is interested in exploring for establishing a national cryptocurrency?

    A. Establishing new banks for the distribution of cryptocurrency services

    B. Disbursing funds through accounts directly linked to the Federal Reserve

    C. Having the Federal Reserve partner with private banks

    D. Claiming eminent domain over crypto currency exchanges and making them an arm of the federal government

2. One of the two main reasons the U.S. government would be interested in legitimizing cryptocurrency is:

    A. To limit the amount of illegal activity

    B. To create a new asset class which it can then use to tax investors

    C. To dispense with the cost of printing paper money and minting coins

    D. To strengthen monetary policy

3. The Cyber Unit is a law enforcement agency of the FOMC. True or false?

    A. True

    B. False

4. Initial Coin Offerings (ICOs) are a concern to the government because:

A. Investors cannot be taxed

B. The potential for fraud is high

C. ICOs are only Bitcoin-based

D. The regulations are onerous to verify

5. The Internal Revenue Service has declared that cryptocurrencies will be regarded as a nontaxable currency. True or false?

A. True

B. False

6. Identify one of the two activities the International Monetary Fund wants to prevent:

A. Financing terrorist activities

B. Providing humanitarian relief

C. Funding the detoxification of the Pacific Ocean

D. Money laundering

7. The Silk Road was:

A. A notorious factory that abused silkworms

B. A road that was paved with coarse silk

C. The 19th century caravan route to China

D. None of the above

Chapter 8: Answers

1. Which of these choices is one of the two possible implementations the United States government is interested in exploring for establishing a national cryptocurrency?

A. Establishing new banks for the distribution of cryptocurrency services

B. Disbursing funds through accounts directly linked to the Federal Reserve

C. Having the Federal Reserve partner with private banks

D. Claiming eminent domain over crypto currency exchanges and making them an arm of the federal government

Answer: B or C are both correct. Disbursing funds through accounts directly linked to the Federal Reserve is one potential course of action. The other option is having the Federal Reserve partner with private banks.

2. One of the two main reasons the U.S. government would be interested in legitimizing cryptocurrency is:

A. To limit the amount of illegal activity

B. To create a new asset class which it can then use to tax investors

C. To dispense with the cost of printing paper money and minting coins

D. To strengthen monetary policy

Answer: A or D are both correct. While B and C are intriguing ideas, the U.S. government is currently interested in curtailing criminal activity and strengthening monetary policy.

3. The Cyber Unit is a law enforcement agency of the FOMC. True or false?

A. True

B. False

Answer: B. False. The Cyber Unit is a law enforcement agency of the Securities and Exchange Commission (SEC), not the Federal Open Market Committee (FOMC).

4. Initial Coin Offerings (ICOs) are a concern to the government because:

A. Investors cannot be taxed

B. The potential for fraud is high

C. ICOs are only Bitcoin-based

D. The regulations are onerous to verify

Answer: B. The Securities and Exchange Commission is concerned that some ICOs may only be offered to the public as a scam for stealing money.

5. The Internal Revenue Service has declared that cryptocurrencies will be regarded as a nontaxable currency. True or false?

A. True

B. False

Answer: B. False. The Internal Revenue Service has stated that cryptocurrencies will be regarded as taxable property.

6. Identify one of the two activities the International Monetary Fund wants to prevent:

A. Financing terrorist activities

B. Providing humanitarian relief

C. Funding the detoxification of the Pacific Ocean

D. Money laundering

Answer: A and D are both correct. Preventing terrorist activities and money laundering are the two main reasons the IMF is working with national governments around the planet.

7. The Silk Road was:

A. A notorious factory that abused silkworms

B. A road that was paved with coarse silk

C. The 19th century caravan route to China

D. None of the above

Answer: D. The Silk Road in the context of cryptocurrency was a black market that used bitcoin to pay for illegal activities.

Chapter 9

Investing in Digital Currencies

Investing in digital currencies is the same as investing in any other category, whether stocks, bonds, commodities... Digital currencies are simply another asset class, and all the careful research you would normally conduct when deciding on whether or not to invest in the stock of a particular company is similar to the amount of due diligence you should perform before committing your resources to a digital currency investment. This chapter will present cautionary advice on how to protect your resources, the steps to take when investing, and the tax implications your investment may incur.

Objectives

In this chapter you will:

- Understand the volatile nature of cryptocurrencies when including them in your investment portfolio.
- Know six essential features when gauging the investment value of a cryptocurrency.
- Learn the basics of how to open a cryptocurrency trading account.

- Find out the names of the four ETFs currently offering stock in blockchain technology.
- Be more informed about how the IRS is responding to cryptocurrency acquisitions, exchanges, and expenditures.
- Identify eight ways the ownership of cryptocurrencies will generate a taxable event.

Managing Cryptocurrency Portfolios

Most investors know the awful feeling of losing a large amount of their paper gains in a short period of time. Unpleasant, scary, creating feelings of doubt and worry...this experience is not uncommon when investing in cryptocurrencies because this asset class is still in its Wild West days. There is no meaningful government regulation and seasoned investors are subject to the influences of untrained and undisciplined first-time investors who are jumping onto digital currency with the enthusiasm of riding a fad with all the thrills of a get-rich-quick scheme.

It's not uncommon to see your paper gains evaporate quickly, and then restore themselves soon after with even more gain, and because of the volatility of this asset class, it's important to be psychologically prepared for rapid inclines and declines. Value can fall quickly due to market manipulation or profit taking, and can also rise quickly on surges of greed.

As with any investment, also approach this market with caution and knowing yourself well as an investor, aware of your foibles and protecting yourself with a well-developed Investment Policy Statement that will guide you intelligently when you may be sorely put with flaring emotions.

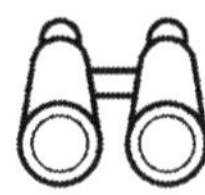

Definition:

Investment Policy Statement: A formal set of rules an investor follows for buying, holding, and selling investments to build wealth and remove the emotions of fear and greed from the trading process.

Whether or not you choose to invest in Bitcoin, because of its influence as a founding coin, always be aware of Bitcoin's circumstances. At this point in the history of digital currencies, Bitcoin's influence will have a palpable effect on the other cryptocurrencies' movement and value, so knowing if Bitcoin is in a bull, consolidation, or bear market should be insightful. Current indicators are that Bitcoins and other alternative coins have an inverse relationship; when Bitcoin's price is rising, the value of the other coins is regressing, and when Bitcoin's value is receding, the value of the other altcoins is rising. This tendency may or may not continue and the cautious investor will carefully review and draw his or her own conclusions.

Key:

When buying, trading, or selling a cryptocurrency, always check what phase Bitcoin is in because the value of altcoins is likely to be in some relation to Bitcoin's movements.

The cryptocurrency market is booming and will continue to do so, and what began in 2009 can't be undone. More and more people are learning about cryptocurrencies and are thinking about investing in them. Some questions people ponder: Is

Bitcoin going to rise even more? Should I invest some money in Ether? What about Litecoin? Which cryptocurrency is the best?

Because conditions can change so rapidly in this highly volatile market, if you're interested with investing here, you should always seek the advice of a financial advisor who has experience with trading in this asset class. The size of your investment should also be limited so losses can be contained within the margin of risk you are willing to accept.

Key:
If you plan to make a large investment in cryptocurrencies, first seek the advice of a financial planner experienced with trading cryptocurrencies.

All the standard investment practices have their continued role to play in your planning and execution. You and your professional financial planner should employ fundamental analysis and technical analysis, set targets within a range between pain and gain, know when to enter a trade and when to exit, employ stop-loss orders...all of this is familiar territory by now.

If you master one exchange it doesn't mean you know them all. Once you begin trading on several different exchanges, you will notice they differ in important ways. Before choosing an exchange, always check the trading platform, method of purchase, liquidity, fee structure, supported tokens, authenticity and security, and user interface and user experience. All of these features and characteristics will have a bearing on your success as a trader or investor.

Note:
Each altcoin has its own characteristics and may make trades differently than the others.

Remember that the unregulated environment of cryptocurrencies has attracted the attention of criminals and con-men since their origin. Evaluate the situation carefully before jumping into uncharted waters, especially with Initial Coin Offerings as you may find yourself unexpectedly swimming with sharks. The best advice is finding a financial planner experienced in cryptocurrency markets and professional asset trading to help you set up a rational investment plan that focuses on limiting your risk while enhancing the potential for your investment's growth.

Valuation

When assessing the value and risk of a cryptocurrency investment, there are specific characteristics of an asset which should be carefully considered. Here are six essential features all investors should carefully review before making a decision to trade or invest.

1. **Market share:** Market share represents the proportion of market capitalization a cryptocurrency possesses in relation to the other cryptocurrencies. The larger the market share, the more dominant the cryptocurrency. These days, Bitcoin has the largest share of total market capitalization in the cryptocurrency category. Market share is a useful indicator for determining the long-term viability of a cryptocurrency in your portfolio.

2. Utility value: The longevity of a cryptocurrency as a viable investment is an important consideration, so its usefulness is an important feature. Is the cryptocurrency useful? Does it have a users' market? The more useful a cryptocurrency is, the more likely it may be widely adopted, thus establishing longevity and investment value over the long term. Ethereum, for example, derives its utility value from its ability to allow developers to build decentralized applications (dApps) on top of its blockchain. It's possible that as long as Ethereum is the main source for dApp development, it is possible to maintain and maybe increase its utility value. Therefore, Ethereum could be a viable cryptocurrency contender to consider including in your portfolio.

Note:
Bitcoin may not have as high a utility value as Ether or Litecoin because, for example, it has a low transaction rate by comparison.

3. Transaction volume: It's one thing to have the potential for use, but quite another to actually be used. Determining if a cryptocurrency is being used can be resolved by looking at its transaction volume. Using Ethereum as an example, its transaction volume is presently over 1,000,000 per day. Historically, this number is increasing, and if this ascending trend continues, Ethereum's long-term viability is positive and could be one reason to maintain it in your portfolio.

4. Technology development: It's clear that technical proficiency is a key component of cryptocurrency trading and investment. If a cryptocurrency's technology is imperfect, there is a strong chance that in the long-term the cryptocurrency will fail. An example of a positive technological development is Ethereum's Byzantium hard fork which allowed the processing of more transactions on the Ethereum blockchain. This technological development increased the likelihood of Ethereum being more widely adopted, continuing to make it a viable candidate for your portfolio.

5. **Public Perception:** The weight of public perception also has a bearing on the value and longevity of a cryptocurrency. When people respond favorably to innovations that enhance some aspect of a cryptocurrency, the favorable public perception imbues that cryptocurrency with additional value. On the other hand, when a cryptocurrency receives negative press, as when the Mt. Gox losses erased millions of dollars of wealth, the public is less likely to favor a cryptocurrency because of the fear of further losses and other inconsistencies.

6. **Supply and Demand:** When a commodity such as oil or gold is in short supply, its value typically increases. The opposite is also true; when a commodity is available in excess, its value retracts. The same dynamic is true for cryptocurrencies. Bitcoin has set a maximum of 21 million coins. With this limited supply, and assuming the coin remains highly regarded by the public, it's safe to conjecture that the value of Bitcoin is likely to increase.

These are six of the predominant factors that influence the value of cryptocurrencies, some of which are significant in assessing the value and risk of other tradeable assets as well.

How to Buy Cryptocurrencies

Exchanges: There are several online exchanges where you can buy cryptocurrencies. One of the currently more popular exchanges is Coinbase which is publicly traded as COIN on the NASDAQ. This exchange is regarded as easy to use and trustworthy, though it has been known to go off-line during particularly frenzied trading. Binance, Crypto.com, Kraken, Bitstamp, ByBit and Gemini are other centralized cryptocurrency exchanges you might look into.

Users can set up an online account from their laptop or download an app to their smart phone. After agreeing to the terms and completing your account, the exchanges typically show charts of the recent trading history of several currencies, and prompts are provided for users to make purchases which usually include connecting a debit or credit card, or adding a direct line to your bank account. A small fee is taken by the exchange for their service and the remaining funds are held in your trading account. Be aware that you may receive a phone call from your bank questioning the authority of your transaction; this happens sometimes with the first transaction as some banks have alerts to protect their members. As your account grows, remember to periodically move excess currency to your cold storage wallet for safekeeping.

Cryptocurrency ETFs: Another way to get involved is through ETFs (exchange traded funds). ETFs offer investors the opportunity to invest in blockchain technology. See Chapter 11 for more information.

Taxes

While the IRS has provided scant direction on the taxation of investments in cryptocurrencies, it's been made clear that the IRS regards Bitcoins and all altcoins as property subject to taxation, even though the general public regards them as virtual currencies. This means that selling, spending, earning, and exchanging cryptocurrencies could result in capital gains or be regarded as taxable income. Here are some examples of the tax implications when buying, selling, or receiving cryptocurrency.

Air drops: Air drops are when free tokens or coins are distributed to the users or owners of a blockchain or cryptocoin. These are considered ordinary income on the day of the air drop. The value on the day of distribution becomes the basis of the coin, and when the coin is sold, exchanged, etc., the result will be a capital gain.

Converting a cryptocurrency to U.S. dollars: When you convert a cryptocurrency and there is a gain, that action becomes a taxable event because the property was sold, generating capital gains or losses.

Exchanging cryptocurrencies: Exchanging one coin for another, such as using bitcoin to purchase ethereum, will create a taxable event. The token is regarded as having been sold, and therefore it generates capital gains or losses.

Initial coin offerings (ICO): The issuance of ICO coins is not categorized under the IRS's tax-free treatment for raising capital. Therefore, the issuance of coins results in ordinary income to individuals and businesses.

Mining coins: When a miner acquires a coin through mining, the newly mined coin is regarded as ordinary income with a value equal to the fair market value on the day the coin was mined.

Receiving payments of cryptocurrencies: Receiving payments of cryptocurrencies for products sold or services provided, or receiving cryptocurrencies as salary, is treated as ordinary income based on the fair market value of the coin at the time of receipt.

Spending cryptocurrencies: When you spend cryptocurrencies, this becomes a taxable event and could generate capital gains or losses. The length of time you hold a coin will determine if it is a short-term or long-term capital gain or loss. An example of this is if you bought a single coin for $50. Should that coin increase in value to $100 and you then purchased a $100 gift card, you will generate a $50 taxable gain. Depending on how long you hold this resource, you could generate either a short or long-term capital gain which would then be subject to different tax rates.

Trading cryptocurrencies: Trading produces capital gains or losses; gains are subject to taxation, and losses may be used to offset gains and reduce tax.

Because there is very little guidance from the IRS, it presently appears the IRS will tax holdings based on the First-In-First-Out treatment. Also, it may make sense to minimize taxes by buying and holding for longer than one year since short-term capital gains are taxed at the ordinary tax rate and long-term gains may have a reduced taxation rate given your bracket. Even so, with cryptocurrency volatility moving the markets like a roller coaster, it could be in your best interest to lock in profits and pay taxes on your gains. Investors should seek guidance from their financial planners, their accountants, and their tax advisors.

Since digital exchanges are not fully regulated by the IRS, tax document preparation is likely to be more complicated in these early years. Exchanges don't issue a 1099 form to report dividends or distributions, and they also do not calculate the capital gains or cost basis for traders.

Note:

The IRS is mindful of cryptocurrencies and their generation of taxable income, so keep accurate records like you would for any other investment.

Cryptotaxation is undefined, and because of this it will be to your advantage to stay ahead of the game rather than finding yourself in a financially uncomfortable circumstance.

It's true that the IRS has been more lenient in the past with taxpayers who volunteer their information than those who prefer the shadows and appear to align with tax avoidance and criminal intent. Current data suggests that very few people are reporting their cryptogains, leading the IRS to adopt a cynical attitude toward the many thousands of investors and traders who have chosen to slip past government scrutiny...for the time being.

Summary

The appeal of investing in a brand-new asset class is compelling, as fortunes will be made in these early days when the industry is as yet unformed, highly flexible, unregulated, and formally untaxed. However, just as there is opportunity for great wealth, so also is there the danger of great loss. Criminal activity in the form of fraudulent ICOs is apparent, and the steady issuance of new cryptocurrencies suggests a potential for instability and short lifespan.

Experienced investors know every investment must be regarded with caution and due diligence, and the protocols for careful review and decisions based on an established and proven Investment Policy Statement along with the cogent advice of a financial planner experienced in cryptocurrency investing should be employed to safeguard wealth and secure measured returns.

Chapter 9: Review Questions

1. Why does the fluctuating value of Bitcoin influence the movement and value of altcoins?

A. Because Bitcoin is a founding altcoin

B. Because the market values Bitcoin as the standard in cryptocurrency value

C. Because altcoins always move in contrast to Bitcoin

D. Because Bitcoin has more market capitalization than all the other altcoins combined.

2. The exchanges that offer investors and traders the opportunity to purchase cryptocurrencies each have their own characteristics, benefits, and detriments. True or false?

A. True

B. False

3. Transaction volume is an important consideration when assessing the value and risk of a cryptocurrency investment because:

A. The number of daily trades maintains cash liquidity

B. Daily trading equates with good management

C. Cryptocurrencies that trade less than 100,000 transactions an hour indicate weak viability

D. High transaction volume demonstrates a cryptocurrency's usefulness

4. You can purchase ETFs that invest in cryptocurrencies. True or false?

A. True

B. False

5. The IRS regards cryptocurrencies as a source of capital gains and losses for taxation purposes. Which of the following are not likely to be taxed?

A. Air drops

B. Converting a cryptocurrency to U.S. dollars

C. Exchanging cryptocurrencies

D. Investment in ICOs

E. Mining coins

F. Receiving payments in the form of cryptocurrencies

G. Spending cryptocurrencies

H. Trading cryptocurrencies

I. None of the above

J. All of the above except Choice I

6. Online exchanges currently do not issue IRS Form 1099, nor do they calculate the capital gains or cost basis for traders. True or false?

A. True

B. False

Chapter 9: Answers

1. Why does the fluctuating value of Bitcoin influence the movement and value of altcoins?

A. Because Bitcoin is a founding altcoin

B. Because the market values Bitcoin as the standard in cryptocurrency value

C. Because altcoins always move in contrast to Bitcoin

D. Because Bitcoin has more market capitalization than all the other altcoins combined

Answer: B. Bitcoin is the standard in cryptocurrency value because it has the most longevity and is regarded as the safest cryptocurrency. Choice A is incorrect because Bitcoin is not an altcoin. Altcoins are defined as all cryptocurrencies created after Bitcoin.

2. The exchanges that offer investors and traders the opportunity to purchase cryptocurrencies each have their own characteristics, benefits, and detriments. True or false?

A. True

B. False

Answer: A. True. If you master one exchange it doesn't mean you know them all. Once you begin trading on several different exchanges, you will notice they differ in important ways.

3. Transaction volume is an important consideration when assessing the value and risk of a cryptocurrency investment because:

A. The number of daily trades maintains cash liquidity

B. Daily trading equates with good management

C. Cryptocurrencies that trade less than 100,000 transactions an hour indicate weak viability

D. High transaction volume demonstrates a cryptocurrency's usefulness

Answer: D. It's a positive sign when a cryptocurrency is being used a lot, as it shows viability and suggests longevity.

4. You can purchase ETFs that invest in cryptocurrencies. True or false?

A. True

B. False

Answer: B. False. ETFs are currently available only for investment companies developing blockchain technology. To date, ETFs are not available for cryptocurrencies.

5. The IRS regards cryptocurrencies as a source of capital gains and losses for taxation purposes. Which of the following are not likely to be taxed?

A. Air drops

B. Converting a cryptocurrency to U.S. dollars

C. Exchanging cryptocurrencies

D. Investment in ICOs

E. Mining coins

F. Receiving payments in the form of cryptocurrencies

G. Spending cryptocurrencies

H. Trading cryptocurrencies

I. None of the above

J. All of the above except Choice I

Answer: I. Choices A – H will all create a taxable event.

6. Online exchanges currently do not issue IRS Form 1099, nor do they calculate the capital gains or cost basis for traders. True or false?

A. True

B. False

Answer: A. True. Cryptocurrency exchanges are not now required to issue these reports to their clients. However, investors should keep accurate records for tax document preparation because even though the IRS has so far provided very little guidance, it is wise to anticipate increased IRS vigilance. Volunteering your cryptocurrency-related tax information now is likely to serve you well later when the IRS more thoroughly scrutinizes your cryptocurrency activities.

Chapter 10

Bitcoin ETFs, a Recent Phenomenon

Bitcoin was launched on January 3, 2009, when its pseudonymous creator, Satoshi Nakamoto, mined the first block of the Bitcoin blockchain, known as the "genesis block." This marked the beginning of the Bitcoin network and the release of the Bitcoin software. Satoshi Nakamoto's true identity remains unknown, as he or they disappeared from the public eye in 2010, leaving the project in the hands of the Bitcoin community. Bitcoin is the first decentralized cryptocurrency, designed to operate as a peer-to-peer digital cash system without the need for intermediaries like banks or governments.

In 2010, bitcoin first became available as a speculative asset and as a digital form of currency. In March 2013, the U.S. Financial Crimes Enforcement Network authorized regulatory guidelines for bitcoin miners, regarding them as money services businesses. Because of its continuing popularity, durability and viability, the Chicago Mercantile Exchange (CME) introduced bitcoin futures as a tradable financial commodity in December 2017.

Bitcoin's market capitalization became $1 trillion in February 2021, and also became legal tender in El Salvador in September 2021. Then, in October 2021, the SEC approved bitcoin ETF futures contracts, which became available on the Chicago Mercantile Exchange. As of this printing, the most recent development occurred in January 2024 when 11 U.S. spot bitcoin ETFs were offered on American stock exchanges for the first time. This measure also received the required approval of the SEC, significantly advancing bitcoin's prominence in domestic and global markets.

Objectives:

In this chapter you will:

- Understand more about how BTC has become increasingly acceptable to traders and investors.
- Consider the difference between investing in BTC through outright purchase of the currency or through an ETF.
- Find out how to purchase spot BTC ETFs.

An Exchange-Traded Fund (ETF) is an investment fund that trades on stock exchanges, combining features of both mutual funds and individual stocks. Managed by professional portfolio managers or designed to track specific indexes, ETFs hold diversified portfolios of assets like stocks, bonds, or commodities. Unlike mutual funds, ETFs are traded continuously throughout the trading day, providing investors with flexibility to buy and sell shares at market prices. This liquidity, coupled with the transparency of daily holdings' disclosure, enables investors to make informed decisions. ETFs often boast lower expense ratios than mutual funds, making them cost-effective investment options, subject to brokerage fees.

ETFs tend to be tax-efficient due to lower portfolio turnover, translating to fewer capital gains distributions. Various types of ETFs cater to different investment needs, including equity ETFs for market index tracking, fixed-income ETFs for bonds, commodity ETFs for tracking commodity prices, international ETFs for global market exposure, and specialty ETFs focusing on specific investment strategies or themes. Overall, ETFs offer investors a convenient and diversified approach to investing in various asset classes with the added benefit of intra-day trading on stock exchanges.

Note:

At the time of this printing, there are 11 spot bitcoin ETFs available through the CME.

The introduction of the 11 new bitcoin ETFs represents a significant development in the cryptocurrency and investment landscapes. These ETFs function similarly to traditional ETFs but are specifically designed to track the price of bitcoin, the most well-known and widely traded cryptocurrency.

Managed by professional portfolio managers or structured to follow specific bitcoin indexes, these ETFs provide investors with a convenient and regulated way to gain exposure to bitcoin without the need to directly hold the digital asset themselves. Unlike buying bitcoin directly on cryptocurrency exchanges, which can involve complex processes and security concerns, investors can now buy and sell shares of bitcoin ETFs through traditional brokerage accounts, offering ease of access and liquidity.

The launch of bitcoin ETFs has attracted significant attention from both retail and institutional investors, indicating growing acceptance and mainstream adoption of cryptocurrencies as investment assets. However, it's essential for investors to conduct thorough research and consider the risks associated with investing in bitcoin and cryptocurrency-related products before making investment decisions.

Now that bitcoin is more ingrained in the financial industry, and with the SEC approval of the 11 spot bitcoin ETFs, there are now 11 exchange-traded funds offering investment opportunities in bitcoin assets, traded on a stock exchange just like any other publicly traded stock. The word "spot" means the day-to-day current bitcoin price, or spot price. Obviously, this has expanded the availability of bitcoin investment opportunities, previously offering only bitcoin ETF futures since 2021 but now also bitcoin spot ETFs since January 2024.

Buy an ETF or Purchase Bitcoin Directly on a Cryptocurrency Exchange?

Selecting the right bitcoin ETF involves careful consideration of several factors to insure the ETF aligns with your investment objectives and risk tolerance. Begin by assessing the ETF's underlying structure, including its tracking methodology and management approach. Evaluate the reputation and credibility of the ETF issuer and ensure regulatory compliance for added security.

Whether buying an ETF or BTC directly, the two choices command different fees and the savvy investor will carefully analyze the expense ratios of each. While cryptocurrency exchanges have one-time fees when buying or selling bitcoin, a bitcoin ETF may also include an annual expense ratio fee, and a trading fee when you choose to sell your ETF. But then, should you own bitcoin on an exchange and choose to transfer your bitcoin from the exchange to a separate crypto wallet, your exchange may assess a small withdrawal fee.

Other elements to consider are liquidity and trading volume to ensure the smooth execution of trades. Research the ETF's historical performance and track record, analyzing factors such as volatility, returns, and risk-adjusted metrics. Assess the fund's transparency, including its holdings and pricing mechanisms, to gain confidence in its operations.

Risk is another important factor. Because bitcoin is a relatively new digital asset and has experienced tumultuous years, wary investors might be more inclined to hedge their risk by purchasing an ETF. Because it appears that bitcoin is here to stay, investing in a bitcoin ETF might be a more conservative way to include bitcoin in your retirement planning.

Other investors may wish to invest more aggressively and own BTC outright, recognizing their potential vulnerability with security issues such as hacking and losing passwords.

Consider seeking advice from financial professionals or conducting thorough due diligence to make informed decisions aligned with your investment strategy and objectives.

Investing in Bitcoin ETFs

If you wish to purchase a spot bitcoin ETF, you must first open a brokerage account with an online brokerage, and there are many from which to choose. Once your account is open, you can purchase bitcoin ETFs in the same manner as you would purchase any other security or ETF. You simply find the ticker symbol in your brokerage interface, enter the amount of shares you wish to purchase, and click "Buy." Remember that ETFs will deduct the annual expense ratio from your account.

Note:

Investing in BTC ETFs is the same process as investing in any other ETF.

When choosing a spot bitcoin ETF, give some consideration to the expense ratio, the ETF's investment strategies, total assets under management, and past performance. Obviously, past performance will be limited for the time being, until the ETF is able to generate a track record. Of course, past performance is not a guarantee of future results.

As with all investments, bitcoin's future and the prognosis for all cryptocurrencies is undetermined. Crypto assets may remain volatile for the time being, so a wise investor carefully considers the risks and rewards, and makes a decision with discretion.

Fiduciary Responsibility

When assessing the suitability of recommending bitcoin and bitcoin ETFs as a Registered Investment Advisor (RIA), several factors must be carefully considered due to the fiduciary duty to act in the clients' best interests. One major concern is the inherent volatility and speculative nature of cryptocurrencies, which may not align with the principle of prudence, particularly for clients with lower risk tolerance.

The evolving regulatory landscape and lack of clear oversight raise questions about the appropriateness of such recommendations. Without robust fiduciary evidence and due diligence processes, recommending these assets could potentially breach fiduciary duties. RIAs must ensure that clients fully understand the risks involved in investing in bitcoin and bitcoin ETFs, as failure to do so may violate the obligation to provide suitable advice. While these assets offer potential opportunities, RIAs must exercise caution and thoroughly evaluate their suitability within the context of each client's unique financial situation and objectives.

In addition to the concerns surrounding the suitability of recommending bitcoin and bitcoin exchange traded funds, it is worth considering the implications of the client's order being non-solicited. By opting for a non-solicited order approach, advisors ensure they do not act with indiscretion when executing trades on behalf of clients. This helps uphold the fiduciary duty to act solely in the client's best interests without any potential conflicts of interest. Non-solicited orders promote transparency and integrity in the advisory relationship, as clients have full control over their investment decisions without undue influence from the advisor. Adopting a non-solicited order approach for bitcoin ETFs further reinforces the commitment to fiduciary responsibility and aligns with the overarching goal of prioritizing client interests above all else.

More About ETFs: Understanding the Hype and History Behind Bitcoin ETFs

By Eryka Gemma

If you follow the digital asset industry, you know that the long-awaited Bitcoin ETF was approved on January 10, 2024 and started trading the following day. The years prior held a lot of excitement surrounding this product and its potential to solidify bitcoin's role as an institutional asset. Now that the dust has settled and we are a year further from that historic day, it's important to take a step back and gain a full understanding of this win for the digital asset industry. Let's look at what an ETF is, the history of Bitcoin ETFs, and the potential effects of this new opportunity for investors.

What Are ETFs?

Exchange-Traded Funds (ETFs) are investment funds traded on stock exchanges. They contain a basket of securities such as stocks, bonds, or commodities. When you invest in an ETF, you essentially invest in all the assets within that fund. ETFs are designed to track specific sectors or commodities, providing investors with exposure to those markets. A familiar example is gold ETFs. Gold ETFs have been in circulation for over 20 years. These funds either directly hold physical gold bullion or use derivatives contracts to gain indirect exposure to gold. For instance:

- **Physical Gold ETFs:** These ETFs hold actual gold stored securely in vaults. Each share represents fractional ownership of the underlying gold.
- **Synthetic Gold ETFs:** Instead of physical gold, they

use derivatives like futures and options contracts to track gold prices. While they lower expenses, they introduce counterparty risk.

The first gold exchange-traded product was a closed-end fund initially focused on providing investors with ownership of both gold and silver bullion. In 2003, the Gold Bullion Securities ETF was launched on the Australian Securities Exchange. This was considered a significant breakthrough and marked the first-time investors could gain exposure to gold through an ETF structure. The bullion price soared significantly in the years that followed.

Between 2004 and 2011, the price of gold experienced a rally.

- In 2004, gold traded around $450 per ounce.
- By August 2011, it had skyrocketed to over $1,820 per ounce.
- This surge amounted to a staggering 346% increase in just seven years.

Now, let's draw a parallel to Bitcoin. If a spot Bitcoin ETF were to mirror gold's historical jump, we could witness a similar phenomenon. Here's the math:

- Bitcoin ETF is approved at a price of $46,000
- Mimicking gold's 346% return, Bitcoin could potentially reach $163,000 per BTC.

Although Bitcoin is a technologically and economically superior product, gold is still a great comparison to make.

The Path to Having Bitcoin ETFs

Spot Bitcoin ETFs have been attempted for over a decade with the Winklevoss twins filing their first attempt on July 1, 2013.

Since then, the SEC rejected their proposal and multiple other proposals due to concerns about the nascent cryptocurrency's market risk.

In December 2017 the CFTC approved a Bitcoin futures product. These contracts allowed investors to bet on the future price of bitcoin without having to buy or sell the actual cryptocurrency. The trading of Bitcoin futures allowed institutions to place bets on the price without having to actually believe in or hold bitcoin. The immediate effects of this futures product were detrimental; the day the futures product was released marked the peak of that period's bull run with a bitcoin price of almost $20,000. There were mixed feelings about this product although it gave a semblance of regulatory clarity for the market; the need for a Spot Bitcoin ETF was highlighted.

The significance of a Spot ETF vs. a futures market is that a Spot ETF requires actual settlement of the underlying asset, forcing the companies offering this ETF to actually hold Bitcoin, which ultimately drives up the price.

On June 16, 2023, BlackRock filed for a spot bitcoin ETF under the name iShares Bitcoin Trust. Although it was just a filing and not an approval from the SEC, the Internet went wild knowing that BlackRock was in the game and approval of the ETF was imminent.

Before BlackRock's filing, at least eight other companies tried and were denied approval.

On January 9, 2024, the SEC's official Twitter account tweeted that the bitcoin ETF was approved. The tweet was deleted several minutes later and SEC Chairman Gary Gensler clarified that the tweet was unauthorized and false. The SEC later said its account was compromised and it would investigate the matter. This false tweet caused about a 4% jump in the bitcoin price, which then immediately dropped back down. Elon Musk's X (formerly Twitter) released a statement stating that "the compromise was not due to any breach of X's systems."

There was a lot of speculation about whether or not this was price manipulation, a disgruntled employee, or a true error, but one thing was for sure: the organization that has mandated itself to "protect investors" against the Web3 world should do better at protecting itself in the Web2 world!

On January 10, 2024, the SEC approved several spot Bitcoin exchange-traded product applications. The approval opened the door for significant capital inflow into Bitcoin. Notable firms like BlackRock, Fidelity, ARK, VanEck and Frankin Templeton along with crypto-native companies, are now in the market. Franklin Templeton even changed their Twitter profile to "Laser Eyes Ben"; the excitement was real.

The SEC had the option to approve as many or as few ETFs as possible, but they chose to approve all the applicants at once. I appreciated this choice because it allowed the investor to decide which firm to choose. The approval of all applicants was a real testament to how free market economics work. We saw the fee structure for each of the providers become significantly lower even before the ETF was officially approved, aiding these firms with staying competitive.

ETF name & symbol	Fee	Notes
Franklin Templeton Digital Holdings Trust (EZBC)	0.19%	N/A.
Bitwise Bitcoin ETF (BITB)	0.20%	Fee waived for first six months of trading or first $1 billion in fund assets, whichever comes first.
VanEck Bitcoin Trust (HODL)	0.20%	N/A.
Ark 21Shares Bitcoin ETF (ARKB)	0.21%	Fee waived for first six months of trading or first $1 billion in fund assets, whichever comes first.
iShares Bitcoin Trust (IBIT)	0.25%	Fee reduced to 0.12% for first 12 months of trading or first $5 billion in fund assets, whichever comes first.
Fidelity Wise Origin Bitcoin Fund (FBTC)	0.25%	Fee waived until Aug. 1, 2024.
WisdomTree Bitcoin Fund (BTCW)	0.25%	Fee waived for first six months of trading or first $1 billion in fund assets, whichever comes first.
Invesco Galaxy Bitcoin ETF (BTCO)	0.25%	Fee waived for first six months of trading or first $5 billion in fund assets, whichever comes first.
Valkyrie Bitcoin Fund (BRRR)	0.25%	N/A.
Grayscale Bitcoin Trust (GBTC)	1.50%	N/A.

Figure 10: Top 10 Bitcoin Spot ETFs by Fee.

Source: Morningstar, January 11, 2024. https://www.morningstar.com/funds/spot-bitcoin-etfs-are-here-should-you-invest

The After-Effects of the Bitcoin ETF Approval

"Buy the Rumor, Sell the News."

The 90 days leading up to the approval had seen approximately a 60% increase in the price of the digital currency. After the ETF was approved, the price dropped quickly. The price went from around $47,000 to about $39,000 in less than two weeks. From a trading perspective, this drop in price was predictable, and according to the metric of the Fear and Greed Index it was clear that the ETF approval marked the occasion as Max Greed.

Those who watch the blockchain flows concluded that a lot of the price drop was attributed to those who were finally able to sell their shares of GBTC. Due to the ETF approval, Grayscale Bitcoin Trust was no longer trading at a discount; the lock-up period was eliminated and investors were finally able to sell their shares and participate with ETFs at lower fees.

However, the launch proved historic:

- By February 27, 2024, Bitcoin's price recovered to $57,000, up 24% since January 10.
- BlackRock and Fidelity's ETFs set records, each capturing $3 billion in AUM within 30 days. This made history as the two most successful launches in history. We have never seen a fund capture $3 billion in AUM within the first 30 days.
- ARK Invest and Bitwise, not brand name giants in finance, followed closely and secured over $1 billion in assets within 45 days.

One year later in January 2025, Bitcoin is stronger than ever according to its most important metrics.

- Hash rate, or the measure of computational power, is at an all-time high, meaning millions of independent miners are dedicating power to uphold the network. Bitcoin doesn't have a CEO or board of directors, yet its combined computing capacity is greater than the data centers of Amazon, Google and Microsoft combined.
- U.S.-traded ETFs collectively hold over 1.25 million Bitcoin, doubling their holdings since January 2024. These ETFs have made Bitcoin accessible to a broader range of investors, allowing participation in the price appreciation of the asset class without the need for direct cryptocurrency ownership or specialized wallets.
- The price of Bitcoin jumped more than 100% in 2024, beating Berkshire Hathway, the S&P 500 and gold.
- The regulatory environment surrounding the digital asset industry has always been a big point of uncertainty but the new administration seems to have created excitement and a positive, more constructive environment.

Where Do We Go from Here?

Now that Bitcoin is officially an institutional asset class, financial advisors are allowed to market it to their clients, including to endowments and pension funds. These advisors will be referencing charts like Figure 11 when sharing with their clients on the possibility of adding Bitcoin to their investment portfolio. The chart is a curiosity because Bitcoin is either the best performing asset in one year, or the least in another; Bitcoin has never been in the middle.

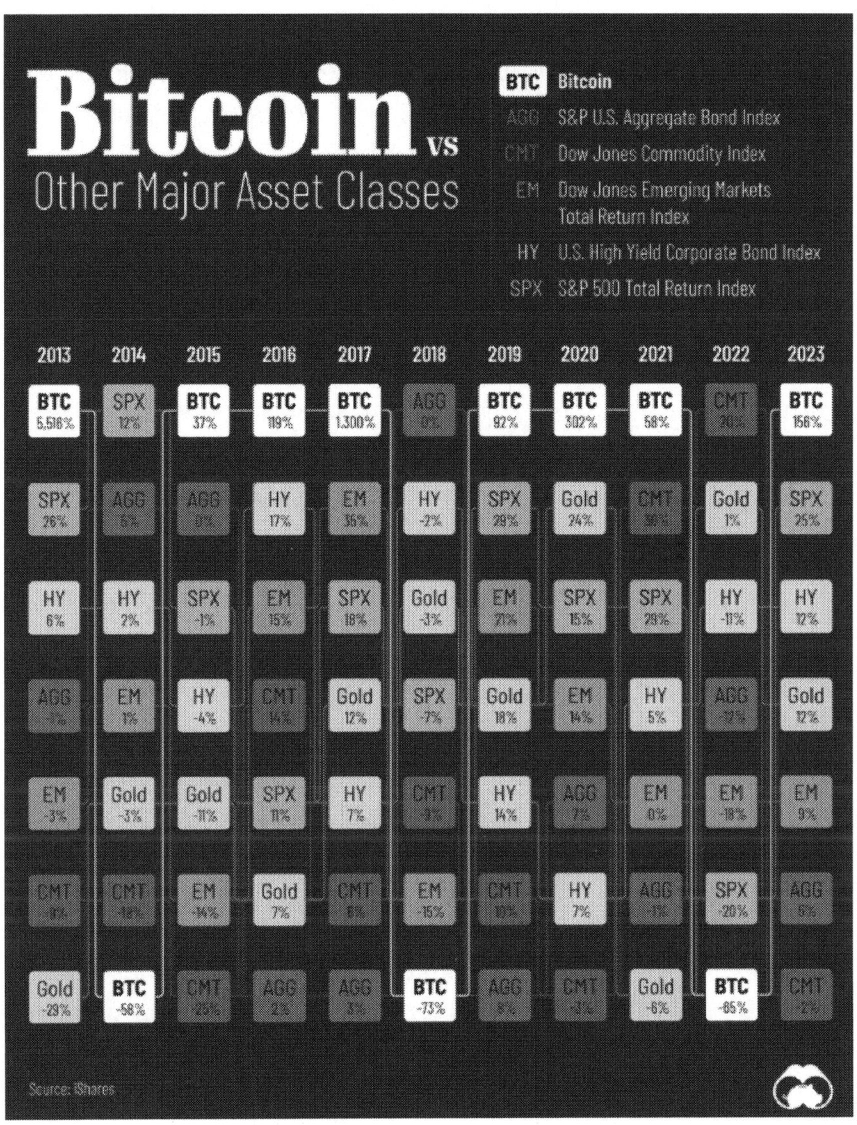

Figure 11: Bitcoin Performance Compared to Major Asset Classes, 2013-2023

Source: Visual Capitalist ((https://www.visualcapitalist.com/bitcoin-returns-vs-major-asset-classes/)

The ETF has now opened the door to an entirely different type of investor. Bitcoin used to be filled with what we call "hodlers", individuals who have an extremely long-time preference and do not sell, no matter the price. This new type of investor is categorized as the portfolio balancing - ratio type. This means that if an investor wants 7% of their portfolio to be allocated to bitcoin, and bitcoin triples in price, this investor will sell to rebalance their portfolio and keep their 7% portfolio requirement. The future is always uncertain, but it will be interesting to see how this new type of investor reacts to bitcoin's volatility ... they may have a lot of constant rebalancing to do!

Looking ahead, Standard Chartered Bank predicts over $100 billion flowing into Bitcoin ETFs in the U.S.; VanEck analysts are also bullish expecting bitcoin prices to reach a high of $180,000 in 2025. Knowing that Bitcoin has a mathematically limited supply, the continuing increase in demand can only be met with price appreciation. While there is excitement about price appreciation, it is clear that the ETF does not fit Satoshi's original vision. There will be an increasing shift from Bitcoin being used as a currency to becoming more of a store of value.

The approval of Bitcoin ETFs marks a significant milestone for crypto adoption. However, as with all markets, only in time will we know the impact of this new investment category of crypto ETFs. For people like me who have been beating the "buy bitcoin" drum for years, it is quite redemptive to say that more people than ever before, including Wall Street, are watching closely and considering this opportunity for growing their wealth.

Summary

With the SEC's approval of spot bitcoin ETFs in January 2024, bitcoin's viability as a legitimate currency was significantly advanced. Because cryptocurrencies are a relatively new asset, and because Bitcoin's early history was tarnished, it has taken over a decade for bitcoin to become established as a bonafide, i.e., governmentally recognized, digital currency.

Private investors and speculators traded bitcoin at first, followed by SEC approval of bitcoin ETF futures in 2021; today, bitcoin spot ETFs are available through the Chicago Mercantile Exchange. It is estimated that as many as 200 million people around the globe currently own BTC, and 420 million people around the world own some form of cryptocurrency.

Chapter 10: Review Questions

1. Which country first adopted bitcoin as legal tender?

A. Costa Rica

B. Columbia

C. El Salvador

D. Bolivia

2. One of the potential difficulties of owning bitcoin outside a managed fund are security issues such as hacking and losing passwords. True or false?

A. True

B. False

3. In 2021, bitcoin's market capitalization was

A. $1 trillion

B. $5 trillion

C. $10 trillion

D. None of the above

4. An exchange traded fund (ETF) is a set of securities designed for a specific outcome, and traded on financial exchanges. True or false?

A. True

B. False

Chapter 10: Answers

1. Which country first adopted bitcoin as legal tender?

    A. Costa Rica

    B. Columbia

    C. El Salvador

    D. Bolivia

    Answer: C. In September 2021, El Salvador was the first country to adopt bitcoin as legal tender.

2. One of the potential difficulties of owning bitcoin outside a managed fund are security issues such as hacking and losing passwords. True or false?

    A. True

    B. False

    Answer: A. True. Digital assets can be vulnerable. People who choose to own bitcoin and other crypto assets must maintain high security.

3. In 2021, bitcoin's market capitalization was

    A. $1 trillion

    B. $5 trillion

    C. $10 trillion

    D. None of the above

    Answer: A. $1 trillion. In 2018, the market capitalization was approximately $128 billion; in 2019, $193 billion; in 2020, $751 billion; and in 2021, $1 trillion.

4. An exchange traded fund (ETF) is a set of securities designed for a specific outcome, and traded on financial exchanges. True or false?

A. True

B. False

Answer: A. True. ETFs can include a varirty of separate stocks, bonds, or commodities. The selection and inclusion of these securities have a defined financial purpose. Currently there are over 8,000 ETFs available worldwide.

Chapter 11

Crypto Asset Insights for Advisors and Their Clients

What RIAs Need to Know for a Crypto-Inclusive Practice

As an RIA or an investor interested by the fascinating and contemporary unfolding of digital assets, it makes sense to identify a structure by which digital assets can be measured for investment potential. This chapter provides a professional overview of current thinking from the CFA Research & Policy Center.

Objectives

In this chapter you will:

- Learn about some of the limitations of this asset sector.
- Consider aspects of valuation approaches.
- Examine assumptions in the crypto category.
- Increase your acumen about misinterpreted variables.
- Decide which models might be appropriate for you and your clients.
- Assess your understanding of crypto assets and consider when you are ready to engage in this sector.

Introduction

The CFA Research & Policy Center's guide, *Valuation of Cryptoassets: A Guide for Investment Professionals*, provides an insightful and thoughtful exploration of the current methodologies for valuing cryptoassets like bitcoin, smart contract platforms, and decentralized applications.

The CFA's paper emphasizes that while existing models offer valuable insights into the mechanics and dynamics of cryptoassets, they remain limited in scope and reliability due to the nascent nature of the crypto ecosystem and the lack of robust historical data. Traditional financial models, such as discounted cash flow (DCF), encounter significant challenges when applied to crypto, given the rapid pace of innovation and the difficulty in defining key assumptions.

The report advocates for a multifaceted, judgment-driven approach to valuation, incorporating various models while remaining open to critique and counter-analysis. This collaborative process, though slow, is essential for the evolution of robust valuation practices that better reflect the unique characteristics of cryptoassets. As the industry matures, continuous research and empirical validation will enhance the understanding and modeling of cryptoassets, laying a stronger foundation for informed investment decisions.

Here follows an overview of valuation methodologies for cryptoassets, derived from traditional finance principles and tailored approaches for this unique asset class. The report emphasizes the need for robust models to guide investment decisions, focusing on three main categories: smart contract platforms, decentralized applications, and Bitcoin.

A. Current Challenges

1. **Lack of Historical Data:** Cryptoassets, being relatively new, have limited data for statistical analysis. This scarcity complicates risk modeling, performance benchmarking, and the development of robust asset allocation strategies. Unlike traditional asset classes with decades of market cycles to analyze, crypto lacks long-term correlations, making it harder to assess its role in a diversified portfolio.

   Also, the evolving regulatory landscape and frequent structural changes in the market further limit the reliability of back-testing and predictive modeling.

2. **Regulatory Gaps:** Uncertainty in regulatory frameworks hinders institutional adoption. The lack of consistent global standards creates compliance challenges, making it difficult for fiduciaries to assess risks and implement crypto strategies confidently. Regulatory agencies continue to debate classifications — whether cryptoassets should be treated as securities, commodities, or something else — leading to fragmented oversight. This uncertainty increases operational and legal risks, deterring broader institutional participation despite growing client interest.

3. **Market Volatility:** Cryptoassets exhibit high price fluctuations, complicating valuation efforts. Unlike traditional assets, their prices are influenced by factors such as regulatory developments, macroeconomic trends, technological advancements, and market sentiment, often leading to rapid and unpredictable swings. This volatility poses challenges for portfolio

allocation, risk assessment, and liquidity planning, requiring RIAs to adopt dynamic strategies and robust risk management frameworks to protect client assets.

B. Valuation Approaches

1. Smart Contract Platforms

- **Network Model:** Valuation considers network effects, using metrics like active users and transaction volume. Metcalfe's Law, which suggests that a network's value is proportional to the square of its users, is a common reference. Beyond user count, transaction velocity, liquidity depth, and the growth of ecosystem applications further refine this approach. Additionally, the security and decentralization of the network play a crucial role, as stronger trust assumptions can drive higher adoption and sustained value accrual.
- **Cash Flow Model:** Platforms are valued as businesses generating revenue from transaction fees (e.g., Ethereum's "gas fees"). Discounted Cash Flow (DCF) models are adapted for intrinsic valuation, though assumptions about network adoption, fee structures, and long-term sustainability introduce complexity.

  Given the volatile nature of crypto markets, sensitivity analysis is critical to account for shifts in user demand, regulatory impact, and evolving competitive landscapes. Additionally, staking yields and token burn mechanisms may affect the overall supply dynamics, influencing future cash flows.

2. Decentralized Applications (dApps)

- **Relative Valuation:** Metrics like price-to-sales and market cap-to-net assets ratios are used to compare within sectors or to traditional finance counterparts. Given the nascency of the dApp ecosystem, additional adjustments may be required to account for token utility, liquidity constraints, and protocol adoption rates. Peer benchmarking within blockchain networks and cross-chain comparisons can also provide insights, though variations in governance models and incentive structures must be carefully weighed. Furthermore, transaction volume and staking yields may serve as alternative valuation inputs, especially in cases where conventional revenue metrics are insufficient.
- **Intrinsic Value:** Protocol revenues, considered as cash flows, form the basis for valuation using growth and discount rate assumptions. These revenues may include transaction fees, staking rewards, or token burn mechanisms that reduce supply over time. Discounted cash flow (DCF) models can be adapted by incorporating crypto-specific risks, such as regulatory uncertainty, network adoption rates, and token velocity effects.

  Additionally, some protocols exhibit quasi-equity characteristics, where governance tokens provide indirect claims on future value accrual, requiring nuanced analysis beyond traditional cash flow projections.

3. Bitcoin

Models Used:

- **Total Addressable Market (TAM):** This approach assesses Bitcoin's potential market size by comparing it to established asset classes, such as gold, which has a market capitalization of approximately $13 trillion. Given Bitcoin's properties as a scarce, non-sovereign store of value, some analysts argue it could capture a meaningful percentage of gold's market share over time. (Aside: Bitcoin's market capitalization is currently $1.9 trillion, about 14% of gold's market capitalization, in February 2025; it was $842 billion in 2024.)

  Additionally, TAM analysis can extend beyond gold to include sovereign wealth reserves, digital payment networks, and alternative assets, refining valuation models based on broader adoption scenarios.

- **Stock-to-Flow:** The Stock-to-Flow (S2F) model for Bitcoin assesses its scarcity by comparing the existing supply (stock) to the annual rate of new issuance (flow). This model posits that the more scarce an asset, the higher its value, with Bitcoin's diminishing supply due to its fixed maximum cap of 21 million coins.

  As the flow (newly mined coins) decreases over time through halving events, the stock-to-flow ratio increases, theoretically driving its price higher. This model is often used to forecast Bitcoin's long-term price appreciation based on the assumption that scarcity correlates directly with value retention, akin to precious metals like gold.

- **Cost of Production:** The cost of production approach evaluates Bitcoin's intrinsic value by analyzing the expenses associated with mining, which include hardware, electricity, and operational costs. This model assumes that the minimum price of Bitcoin should align with the cost to mine it, as miners would be unwilling to operate at a loss.

  Additionally, it factors in network difficulty adjustments and the potential for economies of scale as mining operations grow more efficient over time. While it provides a lower bound for Bitcoin's value, it doesn't fully capture market demand, speculative sentiment, or broader macroeconomic factors that could drive price fluctuations.

- **Limitations:** Each model captures only one aspect of Bitcoin's value proposition, such as its utility as a store of value or medium of exchange. For instance, the stock-to-flow model focuses on Bitcoin's scarcity, while the Metcalfe's Law approach values it based on network effects. However, these models often overlook broader market dynamics, regulatory risks, and adoption rates, all of which can significantly impact its value.

  Consequently, any singular valuation method may fail to provide a comprehensive view, requiring a multifaceted approach that integrates fundamental, technical, and sentiment-based analysis.

C. Key Insights and Metrics

- **Demand-Side Metrics:** Demand-side metrics are crucial for assessing the health and potential of cryptoassets. Active users provide insight into the adoption rate and network engagement, while transaction fees reflect the usage and demand for the asset. Total Value Locked (TVL) indicates the liquidity and ecosystem participation, often used as a barometer for DeFi projects.

  Developer activity, measured by code contributions and project updates, signals the long-term sustainability and innovation within the network. Collectively, these metrics offer a comprehensive view of a cryptocurrency's market demand, adoption, and future growth potential.

- Tokenomics: Tokenomics examines the underlying economic principles governing a cryptocurrency's value, focusing on the mechanisms of supply and demand. It evaluates factors like total token supply, emission schedules, staking yields, and the rate of inflation or deflation, all of which influence scarcity and investor incentives.

  Additionally, the utility of the token within its ecosystem, including governance rights and transaction facilitation, can significantly affect its long-term value proposition. Understanding these dynamics is crucial for assessing a token's sustainability and its potential to generate returns in both bullish and bearish market conditions.

- **Scalability and Efficiency:** Scalability and efficiency are crucial factors when assessing the long-term viability of cryptoassets. Metrics such as transactions per second (TPS) reflect a blockchain's ability to handle high volumes of activity, while average transaction fees offer insight into network congestion and operational costs.

  These indicators are vital for fiduciaries to understand the asset's potential for widespread adoption and its capacity to support real-world use cases efficiently. In addition, lower fees and higher TPS often correlate with better scalability, making these metrics key considerations in portfolio strategy and risk assessment.

D. Limitations of Current Models

Valuation models for cryptoassets often depend on assumptions that can differ significantly between analysts, making consistency a challenge. These models frequently struggle with accurately capturing the speculative nature and market volatility inherent in crypto markets.

Additionally, they may not fully account for external factors like regulatory changes or macroeconomic shifts, which can have disproportionate effects on the value of digital assets. This variability, coupled with the nascent and evolving nature of blockchain technologies, means that valuation estimates are often subject to a high degree of uncertainty, further complicating the fiduciary responsibility of providing reliable financial advice.

A single model cannot fully encapsulate the multifaceted nature of cryptoassets. These assets combine elements of technology, market dynamics, and investor sentiment, which evolve rapidly. Traditional valuation models, rooted in established financial principles, struggle to account for the unique characteristics of cryptocurrencies, such as decentralization, network effects, and regulatory uncertainty.

Additionally, the highly volatile nature of crypto markets further complicates valuation, making reliance on any one method inadequate for accurately assessing their long-term potential and risks. For a comprehensive approach, multiple models should be considered in conjunction to address these complexities.

Ongoing refinements in methodologies are necessary as the industry matures. As blockchain technology and the broader crypto ecosystem continue to evolve, valuation models must adapt to new use cases, governance structures, and asset types. For instance, the emergence of decentralized finance (DeFi), non-fungible tokens (NFTs), and layer-2 solutions introduces complexities that traditional models are ill-equipped to address.

Additionally, as regulatory frameworks take shape, they may significantly impact both market dynamics and the valuation process. Without continuous adjustment, existing models risk mispricing assets or overlooking critical risk factors, highlighting the need for a more dynamic, forward-looking approach.

E. The Report's Conclusion

Cryptoasset valuation remains a complex and evolving field, with various methodologies applied to smart contract platforms, decentralized applications, and bitcoin. However, existing valuation models face significant limitations due to the nascent stage of the crypto ecosystem and the lack of historical data necessary for robust back-testing. Consequently, relying on any single model or metric in isolation is inadequate for accurately determining a cryptoasset's value.

Traditional intrinsic valuation methods, such as discounted cash flow (DCF) models, struggle with the volatility and rapid innovation inherent in the crypto space, making assumption-setting a challenge. Similarly, crypto-specific valuation models, such as those used for bitcoin, often introduce interpretative risks by focusing on select characteristics while neglecting broader market dynamics.

Despite these limitations, the models discussed in the report provide valuable insights into the mechanics and functionality of various cryptoassets. A holistic research approach — one that integrates multiple valuation models with professional judgment and a careful assessment of variables — enhances the decision-making process for investors.

Furthermore, the field benefits from continuous discourse and critical analysis, as disagreement over existing models can lead to refinement and innovation. The introduction of improved valuation frameworks, backed by more comprehensive datasets, will contribute to a better understanding of the factors driving cryptoasset valuation over time.

Ultimately, while no single model can yet offer a definitive valuation framework for cryptoassets, ongoing research and empirical analysis will gradually refine methodologies and establish more reliable market practices. The evolution of valuation models often takes decades, and as the crypto market matures, stronger theoretical foundations will emerge.

The CFA Research & Policy Center's guide, *Valuation of Cryptoassets: A Guide for Investment Professionals*, contributes to that progress, highlighting the importance of developing and testing new models to deepen collective knowledge and improve investment decision-making in the crypto space.

F. Recommendations for Investment Professionals

1. **Diversify Your Frameworks:** Employ multiple valuation frameworks to gain a comprehensive understanding of a crypto asset's potential.
2. **Eductation:** Stay informed on regulatory developments and emerging valuation models.
3. **Use of Tools:** Leverage on-chain analytics to assess the real-time performance and health of blockchain platforms.

Summary: The Top 10 Key Points

1. **Valuation Challenges:** Current cryptoasset valuation models face limitations due to the sector's early-stage development and lack of comprehensive historical data.
2. **Diverse Asset Types:** The paper focuses on valuation approaches for bitcoin, smart contract platforms, and decentralized applications, each requiring unique considerations.
3. **Limitations of Traditional Models:** Intrinsic valuation techniques like DCF models face difficulties

in crypto due to sensitivity to assumptions and limited applicability.

4. **Crypto-Specific Models:** Models tailored to cryptoassets, such as bitcoin-specific frameworks, can suffer from misinterpreted variables and an overemphasis on certain features.

5. **Insights into Functionality:** Despite their limitations, existing models provide valuable insights into the mechanics and dynamics of cryptoassets.

6. **Holistic Approach:** A balanced methodology combining multiple models and professional judgment yields better investment decisions than relying on a single model.

7. **Embracing Disagreement:** Critiquing and debating existing models fosters innovation and leads to more robust valuation frameworks.

8. **Future Improvements:** As more data becomes available and crypto markets mature, valuation models will evolve and become more reliable.

9. **Long-Term Process:** The development of widely accepted valuation methodologies is a gradual process that could take decades.

10. **Research Contribution:** This report serves as a vital step in enhancing collective understanding and advancing the modeling capabilities for cryptoassets.

Chapter 11 Questions

1. True or False? The CFA Research & Policy Center's guide argues that existing valuation models for cryptoassets are both comprehensive and reliable due to the extensive historical data available.

   A. True

   B. False

2. Which of the following is a significant challenge in valuing cryptoassets?

   A. Excessive historical data leading to overfitting in predictive models

   B. The lack of long-term correlations and historical data

   C. The low market volatility of cryptoassets

   D. Overregulation and excessive government oversight

3. True or False? The guide suggests that regulatory uncertainty and the lack of consistent global standards pose significant challenges for institutional adoption of cryptoassets.

   A. True

   B. False

4. Which valuation approach is commonly applied to smart contract platforms using network effects as a metric?

   A. Cost of Production

B. Relative Valuation

C. Network Model

D. Discounted Cash Flow

5. True or False? The Stock-to-Flow model values Bitcoin based on its transaction volume and liquidity rather than scarcity and supply constraints.

A. True

B. False

6. Which of the following factors is NOT mentioned as a key driver of market volatility in cryptoassets?

A. Regulatory developments

B. Macroeconomic trends

C. Fixed supply of cryptoassets

D. Market sentiment

7. True or False? The report advocates for a singular, rigid valuation model to improve accuracy in assessing cryptoassets.

A. True

B. False

8. The Total Addressable Market (TAM) approach to valuing Bitcoin compares it primarily to which asset?

A. Real estate

B. Gold

C. Government bonds

D. Oil reserves

9. True or False? One limitation of current cryptoasset valuation models is that they may struggle to account for external factors such as regulatory changes and macroeconomic shifts.

A. True

B. False

10. Which of the following is a key insight emphasized in the guide regarding cryptoasset valuation?

A. Demand-side metrics, such as active users and transaction fees, are critical for assessing network health

B. The most accurate valuation model for Bitcoin is the Cash Flow Model

C. Cryptoasset valuation is best approached using a single, well-established financial model

D. Scalability and efficiency play little role in determining the long-term viability of cryptoassets

Chapter 11: Answers

1. True or False? The CFA Research & Policy Center's guide argues that existing valuation models for cryptoassets are both comprehensive and reliable due to the extensive historical data available.

    A. True

    B. False

    Answer: B. False. The guide acknowledges that existing models offer insights but remain limited due to the nascent nature of the crypto market and the lack of historical data.

2. Which of the following is a significant challenge in valuing cryptoassets?

    A. Excessive historical data leading to overfitting in predictive models

    B. The lack of long-term correlations and historical data

    C. The low market volatility of cryptoassets

    D. Overregulation and excessive government oversight

    Answer: B. The lack of long-term correlations and historical data. A key challenge in crypto valuation is the lack of historical data, which makes statistical analysis and back-testing difficult.

3. True or False? The guide suggests that regulatory

uncertainty and the lack of consistent global standards pose significant challenges for institutional adoption of cryptoassets.

A. True

B. False

Answer: A. True. Regulatory uncertainty and the lack of global standards hinder institutional adoption and increase operational risks.

4. Which valuation approach is commonly applied to smart contract platforms using network effects as a metric?

A. Cost of Production

B. Relative Valuation

C. Network Model

D. Discounted Cash Flow

Answer: C. Network Model. The Network Model values smart contract platforms based on network effects, often using Metcalfe's Law.

5. True or False? The Stock-to-Flow model values Bitcoin based on its transaction volume and liquidity rather than scarcity and supply constraints.

A. True

B. False

Answer: B. False. The Stock-to-Flow model focuses on Bitcoin's scarcity by comparing existing supply to the annual issuance rate.

6. Which of the following factors is NOT mentioned as a key driver of market volatility in cryptoassets?

A. Regulatory developments

B. Macroeconomic trends

C. Fixed supply of cryptoassets

D. Market sentiment

Answer: C. Fixed supply of cryptoassets. While Bitcoin's fixed supply affects its long-term value, the guide attributes volatility more to regulatory developments, macroeconomic trends, and market sentiment.

7. True or False? The report advocates for a singular, rigid valuation model to improve accuracy in assessing cryptoassets.

A. True

B. False

Answer: B. False. The report recommends a multifaceted approach rather than a singular model due to the complexity of crypto valuation.

8. The Total Addressable Market (TAM) approach to valuing Bitcoin compares it primarily to which asset?

A. Real estate

B. Gold

C. Government bonds

D. Oil reserves

Answer: B. Gold. The Total Addressable Market (TAM) approach compares Bitcoin's potential market size primarily to gold.

9. True or False? One limitation of current cryptoasset valuation models is that they may struggle to account for external factors such as regulatory changes and macroeconomic shifts.

A. True

B. False

Answer: A. True. One limitation noted in the report is that valuation models may fail to fully account for external factors like regulation and macroeconomic shifts.

10. Which of the following is a key insight emphasized in the guide regarding cryptoasset valuation?

A. Demand-side metrics, such as active users and transaction fees, are critical for assessing network health

B. The most accurate valuation model for Bitcoin is the Cash Flow Model

C. Cryptoasset valuation is best approached using a single, well-established financial model

D. Scalability and efficiency play little role in determining the long-term viability of cryptoassets

Answer: A. Demand-side metrics, such as active users and transaction fees, are critical for assessing network health. Demand-side metrics, such as active users and transaction fees, are emphasized as crucial indicators of a cryptoasset's health and adoption potential.

Chapter 12

Liquid Real Estate

Would you like to invest in a $10 million property? In our new Digital Age, you don't need to have 20% down ($2 million) or millionaire-level resources that guarantee the mortgage payments. All you really need to do is find a blockchain that holds real estate property and accepts cryptocurrency tokens as the medium of exchange between buyers and sellers.

The concept of liquid real estate is now a new and exciting reality that changes the basic paradigms of the real estate market. You can be a part owner of million-dollar properties by purchasing tokens that represent shared ownership. You can select the property you wish to co-own, and can purchase as much of it as you wish or can afford. As the property appreciates or depreciates in value, the value of your cryptocurrency tokens also appreciate or depreciate, just as if you owned the real estate in the traditional way. Be prepared to learn how you can invest in real estate around the world through blockchain and cryptocurrency technology.

Objectives

In this chapter you will:

- Learn how to buy shares in properties around the globe through liquid real estate tokens.
- Realize how the real estate market is employing blockchain technology and cryptocurrencies to buy and sell real estate.
- Know why the traditional real estate market obstacles to purchase and sale are no longer concerns in the liquid real estate market.
- Understand how a real estate property becomes its own market and is not dependent on the pairing of the buyer and the seller.
- Become familiar with some of the intricacies of an Initial Real Estate Offering (IREO).
- Identify two ways you can participate in the purchase of liquid real estate.
- Find out which type of real estate is a good example of a desirable property in the catalog of a blockchain real estate investment company.
- Discover why a cash down payment and evidence of the ability to make monthly mortgage payments is no longer a necessity.
- Be inspired by why the “double coincidence of wants” is no longer a factor in real estate transactions.

Most investors, having considered the various means by which they can increase their wealth, have recognized the incredible capacity of real estate to provide large returns over a short period of time.

Of course, the blade is sharpened on both sides as one can also lose their fortune with a misplaced purchase; this is the risk every investor accepts when placing their cash on the line.

Even so, real estate has repeatedly proven to be a precious asset, one that is much desired and may fit appropriately in your investment portfolio as an alternative asset. One of the special benefits of owning real estate is that it may also produce income through a leased arrangement, in addition to its potential for appreciation.

The Obstacles to Owning Real Estate: Most people would relish owning a desirable high-priced property but are unable to afford the down payment and the lender's requirement for either collateral or evidence of the buyer's ability to make guaranteed mortgage payments. In addition, money that's invested in property may remain tied up for years, even decades, and liquidating the invested cash can be onerous.

Definition:

Double coincidence of wants. A term stating that a transaction requires both a simultaneous buyer and seller.

If you found an apartment complex that's on the market for $3 million and it has a net operating income of $300,000 per year, this could be an attractive investment...but the opportunity might be completely out of your range.

Even if you could afford to purchase the property, there's always the chance you could wind up in a situation where you needed to access your investment dollars and would have to sell quickly, possibly taking a loss to extricate yourself.

These are conundrums of the past because you have the good fortune of living in the Digital Age where real estate is now available to you at a price you can afford and with complete and instant liquidity. You can choose to continue doing things the old-fashioned way, or you could step into the 21st century of real estate investment.

The Benefits of Tokenizing Real Estate

In prior chapters we've considered the meaning of money and how it transfers between people for the full gamut of goods and services exchanged between people and institutions managed by people. The words we use to describe our various forms of money are myriad and include such labels as dollars, yen, banknotes, Treasury bonds, gift cards, laundromat tokens, amusement park tickets, parking lot permits, electronic bridge tolls, and more. In a sense, these are all tokens representing monetary value, and they are exchanged with other people or agencies who also accept and use these tokens according to their represented and purposed value.

Now the time has come, for it is already here, when real estate properties can also be tokenized, i.e., a real estate property can represent a precise agreed-upon value that can be represented by a certain number of tokens.

The $3 million apartment complex can be split into 3,000,000 real estate tokens specific to this exact property.

Note:

There are many forms of tokens representing monetary value in use today. Liquid real estate tokens are now another version.

In a sense, this is no different than a publicly traded company that sells its 3,000,000 shares at $1 each. Depending on an investor's assessment of the company's prospects, 10,000 shares could be purchased for $10,000 plus fees and the investor would own a percentage of the company. In the same manner, a real estate investor could purchase 10,000 tokens for $10,000 plus fees and own a percentage of the property.

Liquidity: One of the potential headaches with owning real estate is that it may be disagreeably illiquid, preventing the owner from accessing its full cash value when needed. Selling property requires the "double coincidence of wants" which is a term describing the opposing desires of two people, in this case the interest of one to sell the property and the interest of another to purchase it. These two opposing desires must also be simultaneous.

Key:

Now you can invest in expensive properties around the globe without needing large capital resources.

When trading shares of the major domestic market indices like the Dow Jones Industrial Average or NASDAQ, millions of shares are traded daily. However, when trying to sell the apartment building on the corner of 4th Street and Vine, there might only be a handful of prospects. Because there is the possibility of delayed egress from property ownership, an illiquidity discount sometimes lowers the price of a property to attract sufficient prospects with the intention of consummating a sale. Investors with a long-term view and bank accounts full of cash can tolerate holding property that's temporarily illiquid; small-scale investors must be wary.

In this new age of digital investment, however, investors could choose to purchase small amounts of an offered property, even just a few dollars per transaction, and they have the capability of instantly withdrawing all of their investment at a moment's notice if they choose. Blockchain real estate investing offers expanded opportunities and the freedom of instant liquidity. Wow, huh?

How to Invest in Liquid Real Estate

Plan A: Find an Existing Real Estate Blockchain: The easiest way to get involved with owning liquid real estate is to find a real estate blockchain and follow the protocols for establishing an account, transferring cash to your account so you can purchase the amount of tokens you wish to invest in real estate, identify a property that's the best investment for your situation, spend your cryptocurrency tokens to purchase the amount of value you wish to own in that property, and then periodically monitor your investment to determine if this investment is worth retaining or releasing, like any other investment you would make.

Definition:
Initial Real Estate Offering (IREO). The initial proposal of a real estate property available for purchase to attract investors participating in a blockchain real estate network using cryptocurrency.

Plan B: Sponsor a Property for Purchase: Your other choice is to identify an investment company that will allow you to sponsor a property on their real estate blockchain platform so you can propose the purchase of a property to potential co-owners who are members of the investment company's network. Taking the trouble to go through a series of five steps could result in your receiving a nice payout for your efforts, as well as a stake in the property's appreciation if you also choose to be one of the co-owners in the property's blockchain network.

Key:
If you are the sponsor of a property, you could earn a good commission when the property you sponsor is purchased and listed for trading.

Here are the five steps to sponsoring a property:

Step 1: Finding a Property. We advise that you work with a real estate professional to identify properties you believe have strong investment potential. Many liquid real estate property investors are especially interested in properties that generate income through leases and rentals. Follow through with your research and gather all the details you would normally gather as if you are making the investment on your own, for yourself. Once you've established that this property is desirable and would likely be desirable to other co-owners, meet with a representative of a real estate block chain investment company. We can refer you to the one that we work with, if requested.

Step 2: Set-Up an Initial Real Estate Offering (IREO). The next step is to make an offer on the property based on funding contingency. Once the seller accepts your offer, follow the protocols for listing the property in the investment company's catalog of eligible properties. You'll be asked to fill-in the various fields in the online property information form, and complete other related documentation and due diligence.

The process will request you set a "funding goal", which is the amount of capital required to complete the purchase. Using the earlier example, you will need $3 million plus about an additional $600,000 which will cover closing costs, put 10% into a reserve account that's part of the value of the asset, pay a 0.25% platform fee to the host company, and reward you for your efforts.

Because the property creates rental income, and based on the appreciation potential of the property, you predict the property will be worth $4,250,000. This should be well-received by potential co-owners as a desirable investment. You will also need to identify, interview, and select a property management company who will act as the property's trustee; their compensation will come from the rental income generated by the property.

Step 3: Funding the IREO. Now that the property's information is published in the investment company's online catalog, investors will be able to examine the documents, photographs, videos, paperwork, and other descriptive materials about the property to decide if this is a suitable investment for their needs.

Note:
Until the property is purchased, it is being held for only a limited time pending funding.

All members of the investment company's network can now buy as much of the offered property as they choose, using their cryptocurrency tokens. The company we work with does not have any minimum investment requirements, nor do they restrict the number of investors who want to participate. This allows a more accelerated funding of the listed properties. In a sense, this is like a crowd sale with investors choosing to fund one or any of the properties in the catalog in which they wish to invest.

Once the full amount of the purchase price has been secured through the investments made by co-owners with their real estate cryptocurrency tokens, the IREO enters Step 4. If the property is not funded, all investors receive a full refund.

Step 4: Purchasing the Property. Until now, the property has only been held by an accepted offer. Since the funding has been collected from a group of willing investors, the property's purchase must now begin, including related tasks:

1. The sponsor must transfer the $3 million and closing costs to the escrow company to secure the deal.

2. $300,000 (10%) is put into a reserve account. This sum provides the initial liquidity that permits the

immediate sale of investors' tokens for investors who want to cash-out in part or in full.

3. The platform and maintenance fee of 0.25% is paid to the blockchain investment company.

4. The sponsor is paid approximately $150,000 (5%) for arranging the opportunity.

5. The property management company receives their negotiate payment from the income the property generates monthly.

6. Rental income generated by the property is applied to the asset value of the property and is not distributed to the co-owner/investors until they choose to sell their tokens, which is equivalent to selling part or all of their ownership.

Once the property has been purchased, the sponsor is relieved of his or her obligations. If the sponsor was also an investor, then he or she receives the prorated portion of the property's appreciation as time passes.

Step 5: Offering the Property as a Tradeable Asset. Now that the property is owned by any number of investors who purchased tokens on this specific property, and held in trust by the real estate blockchain investment company, the property becomes a tradeable asset through the investment company's technology platform.

New investors can purchase cryptocurrency tokens for this specific property and also become fractional owners. Should the property prove to be a truly worthy investment, its value could increase in three separate ways:

1. Appreciation of the property as a typical real estate property would normally appreciate based on the traditional market standards of assessment.

2. Value growth through the steady rental income that is reinvested into the property's reserve balance each month.

3. Capitalization growth created by new investors who want fractional ownership and invest tokens to do so.

Investors are able to purchase and sell their real estate tokens just as they would buy and sell shares of stock, but the difference is they can now do so whether or not anyone else is willing to buy or sell at the same time. The dynamic of the "double coincidence of wants" no longer applies. Illiquidity is not an issue anymore.

Key:
The pairing of a buyer and seller is no longer a necessity because the property has a reserve that allows instant transactions.

Because the property has become its own market and has the ability to provide instant liquidity of ownership, investors are able to sell their fractional ownership whenever they wish, even when no one is interested in buying the ownership tokens they are selling.

The benefits of tokenizing real estate are:

1. Real estate assets are available for all types and prices of properties.

2. Assets are available in the global marketplace.

3. There is no illiquidity risk, so there is no need for property devaluation to attract prospects and no

discount is needed so the value is preserved.

4. Investors can liquidate their ownership instantly.

5. Investors can purchase ownership instantly.

6. The asset is its own market because it is not dependent on buyers or sellers to determine its value; its value exists independent of buyers and sellers that would normally cause fluctuations in its price, as with stock trading.

Liquid Real Estate Example

A desirable piece of property has been purchased by 360 investors, each purchasing 10,000 tokens valued at $1 each, resulting in a total of $3,600,000. This money was held in escrow and then used to purchase the property. Funds have been disbursed as described above and now the property has been placed on the real estate blockchain investment company's platform, visible in the online catalog and available for trading.

The property is so compelling that none of the 360 fractional owners want to sell their tokens. In the traditional real estate market, other investors who are interested in buying this property are out of luck and unable to get in on this fantastic opportunity.

However, under this new design for real estate investing, investors who missed the initial opportunity can still get involved and also purchase tokens, becoming fractional owners. These new funds are put into the property's cash reserve, and as this reserve increases, it affects and increases the value of the original owners' tokens. As new investors choose to be fractional co-owners, purchasing investment tokens cost more than $1 each, and could be priced at $1.01, or similarly.

As more investors purchase tokens, the value and purchase price of each token rises and falls depending on the inflow and outflow of the investments or withdrawals made by buyers and sellers. Should an investor decide to sell his or her tokens, the process occurs in reverse. The tokens that are sold are destroyed and the representative amount of cash is paid out to the seller who is now no longer a fractional co-owner. The property is its own market.

Key:
Normally, in a traditional real estate sale, new buyers would have to find a seller. With liquid real estate, new buyers can always buy shares of the property because new shares can always be created.

If you're interested in the concept of owning liquid real estate, feel free to contact us. We work with a company using the Ethereum blockchain, providing clients with the opportunity to either purchase liquid real estate property that's already on its own dedicated blockchain and available through their online catalog of properties, or they will also assist you so you could potentially make even more money as the sponsor of an Initial Real Estate Offering (IREO) on their platform.

Summary

As we have seen repeatedly, the combined application of blockchains and cryptocurrency are changing our perceptions of how traditional financial and trading systems can be modified to improve networks of value exchange.

When it comes to real estate, the foregoing information and description illustrates how new opportunities for real estate investing are available.

The challenge of gathering sufficient capital to purchase property or make and justify a mortgage is now antiquated; the issue of having to accept the potential illiquidity of real estate that mandates the possibly lengthy ownership which ties up financial capital until a seller is willing to negotiate and purchase is relegated to a 20th century practice; the requirement of fulfilling the demands of a "double coincidence of wants" is newly soporific; the excessive investment of time and labor expended while researching myriad real estate properties to find suitable prospects for singular investment is now consigned as a recognition of an irrelevant misuse of valuable resources; and possessing the capability of becoming a fractional owner in properties around the globe by engaging in the digital transference of investment capital through tokens controlled from the convenience of a laptop screen is only the beginning of a new vision for real estate entrepreneurs excited by the opportunities now beginning to beckon.

Chapter 12: Review Questions

1. In a listed liquid real estate property, you can purchase:

A. A limited number of shares

B. As many shares as you wish

C. No more than 20% of the available shares

D. 20% of the value of the appraisal

2. Tokens represent a variety of monetary values for such goods and services as amusement park tickets, laundromat coins, freeway lane credits, and restaurant gift cards.

A. True

B. False

3. Which of the following are traditional obstacles to buying real estate?

A. Ability to pay a large cash mortgage

B. Ability to provide evidence of meeting mortgage payments

C. Ability to arrange the double coincidence of wants

D. All of the above

4. With liquid real estate, the "double coincidence of wants" is still an issue because for every buyer, there must also be a seller.

A. True

B. False

5. Which of the following is not a benefit of liquid real estate?

A. Price discount for illiquidity is mandatory

B. New buyers can purchase shares in a property after the initial real estate offering even if none of the original buyers wishes to sell their shares

C. Investors can liquidate their shares instantly

D. All of the above

6. Being the sponsor of a liquid real estate property create a sizable commission.

A. True

B. False

7. IREO are the initials for:

A. Instant Real Estate Opportunity

B. Investment in Real Estate Options

C. Increasing Real Estate Ownership

D. Initial Real Estate Offering

8. The property "has become its own market" means the traditional simultaneous pairing of a seller with a buyer is no longer necessary because buyers can buy shares and sellers can sell shares instantly and independently of each other.

A. True

B. False

9. The IREO's "funding goal" is set higher than the income property's purchase price because the funding goal also includes:

A. A commission for the sponsor

B. Funds for the property management company

C. A 10% reserve fund

D. Closing costs

E. A 0.25% platform fee for the host company

F. Choices A, B, D, E

G. Choices A, C, D, E

10. Tokens sold by co-owners wishing to divest are:

A. Re-sold to new buyers

B. Sold to current co-owners

C. Destroyed so they cannot be reused

D. Added to the cash reserve

Chapter 12: Answers

1. In a listed liquid real estate property, you can purchase::

A. A limited number of shares

B. As many shares as you wish

C. No more than 20% of the available shares

D. 20% of the value of the appraisal

Answer: B. You can buy as many shares as you wish. There is no limit because new tokens will be created to accommodate your investment decision.

2. Tokens represent a variety of monetary values for such goods and services as amusement park tickets, laundromat coins, freeway lane credits, and restaurant gift cards.

A. True

B. False

Answer: A. True. The use of tokens is widespread in our society today.

3. Which of the following are traditional obstacles to buying real estate?

A. Ability to pay a large cash mortgage

B. Ability to provide evidence of meeting mortgage payments

C. Ability to arrange the double coincidence of wants

D. All of the above

Answer: D. All of the above are traditional obstacles to buying real estate. With liquid real estate, these are no longer blocking issues.

4. With liquid real estate, the "double coincidence of wants" is still an issue because for every buyer, there must also be a seller.

A. True

B. False

Answer: B. False. Because the property becomes the market, having a simultaneously interested buyer and seller is no longer a requirement for the buying and selling of shares in a property.

5. Which of the following is not a benefit of liquid real estate?:

A. Price discount for illiquidity is mandatory

B. New buyers can purchase shares in a property after the initial real estate offering even if none of the original buyers wishes to sell their shares

C. Investors can liquidate their shares instantly

D. All of the above

Answer: A. Because the property is its own market, the perceived value of the property is sufficient to attract buyers and there is no reason to discount the price because buyers either will or won't be interested in purchasing shares.

6. Being the sponsor of a liquid real estate property create a sizable commission.

A. True

B. False

Answer: A. True. One of the benefits of being a sponsor is the possibility of earning a large commission once the property is tradeable on the investment company's platform.

7. IREO are the initials for:

A. Instant Real Estate Opportunity

B. Investment in Real Estate Options

C. Increasing Real Estate Ownership

D. Initial Real Estate Offering

Answer: D. The Initial Real Estate Offering (IREO) is the presentation of a property proposed for purchase by co-owners through the blockchain investment company's platform.

8. The property "has become its own market" means the traditional simultaneous pairing of a seller with a buyer is no longer necessary because buyers can buy shares and sellers can sell shares instantly and independently of each other.

A. True

B. False

Answer: A. True. The perceived value of the liquid real estate property drives price, and because the property has a cash reserve for sellers to instantly sell their shares, the pairing of the simultaneous double coincidence of wants is not a necessity in liquid real estate transactions.

9. The IREO's "funding goal" is set higher than the income property's purchase price because the funding goal also includes:

A. A commission for the sponsor

B. Funds for the property management company

C. A 10% reserve fund

D. Closing costs

E. A 0.25% platform fee for the host company

F. Choices A, B, D, E

G. Choices A, C, D, E

Answer: G. All of the listed factors are part of the funding goal except for choice B, as funds for the property management company are paid from rental income.

10. Tokens sold by co-owners wishing to divest are:

A. Re-sold to new buyers

B. Sold to current co-owners

C. Destroyed so they cannot be reused

D. Added to the cash reserve

Answer: C. When the sellers cash out their tokens, their tokens are destroyed as they have lost their value and purpose.

Chapter 13

The Future of Blockchain Technologies and Cryptocurrencies

As we advance further into the dawn of the Digital Age with more technological advances in all elements of our personal and business lives, the comprehensive effect is expected to be profound.

As smart phones have become ubiquitous and laptops have replaced desktop models, as our cars become key-less and capable of parking themselves, as our morning coffee is made by a robot and our refrigerators can be restocked with online orders that bring packages to our doorstep today, and, possibly, delivered some day soon through the assistance of food market drones, we can only imagine how digital currency will continue to morph until it reaches a new status quo of accepted presence in our digital wallets and daily lives.

This chapter gives some idea of where we may be headed as blockchains and cryptocurrencies steadily transform our culture and society into new realms that once resided only on the science fiction pages of our youth.

Objectives

In this chapter you will:

- Realize why blockchains and cryptocurrencies are not like the "tulip mania" of the 17th century.

- Understand the basic risks of purchasing cryptocurrencies.
- Learn about the growing but still limited number of academic studies on blockchains and cryptocurrencies.
- Be introduced to several famous proponents of blockchain technology and cryptocurrencies.
- See how several corporations are using or planning to use this new technology.

There is a human propensity to skeptically regard the current advances of blockchains and cryptocurrencies as the newest fad or latest madness, with cynics comparing this heightened public interest to the Dutch "tulip mania" of the 17th century.

Note:
The tulip mania is the first recorded speculative bubble, occurring circa 1634.

The comparison is without merit because the speculative nature of the tulip bulbs was not based on sound value; the tulips were novel and purchased in quantities until they became momentarily rare, resulting in access is beyond their true value without reasonable cause, eventually succumbing to the unfortunate realization that the tulips were more a curiosity than a true rarity as many people lost their life savings and homes.

A more likely assessment of the future of blockchain and cryptocurrencies would be comparing their advent to the mid-1980s when bulky desktop computers with floppy disks began materializing in offices and homes around the globe, which in turn led to enthusiastically adopting the use of a conduit connecting all the cumbersome boxes to each other, leading to the multi-user digital interconnectivity of the superhighway we know today as the Internet. Who saw that coming?

So, by extension, who can see the potential for blockchain technology and cryptocurrencies exiting the realm of the innovative and entering instead the realm of the visionary? For so it will come to pass...based on the continually increasing interest, participation, and development in our ways of thinking and evolving adoptive practices.

The clever but careful investor will realize blockchain technology is here to stay, and will also acknowledge that many of today's cryptocurrencies may go no further than merely existing as a speculative curiosity, following shortly in the steps of the mighty mammoths, while others will assume a comprehensive role in the financial fabric weaving through our daily monetary exchanges without more thought as a modern-day miracle than we bequest to the eternal passage of clouds in the sky.

Whether it's bitcoin or ether or some other device we accept as currency, there is no question that digital currency, and cryptocurrency in particular, is here to stay. The advantages of Bitcoin may be the source of its immortality, or this digital grandfather may succumb to the more virile and agile characteristics of a cryptocurrency that will yet be invented. Whether investors choose to place their sums in the stock of Edsel or a quirky youngster named Microsoft is the choice that will build the fortunes of many or stockpile mountains of rueful reflection for others decades from now.

Bitcoin was created to exist outside national fiat currencies because of the concerns of technical wizards who saw a way to advance their own fortunes by moving currency beyond the perceived pernicious control of central banks and manipulative politicians. Bitcoin is popular in countries like Zimbabwe and Venezuela where fiat currencies are losing their value because of hyperinflation. Bitcoin is popular there also because transactions can be conducted on smart phones making it easy to transact business and make simple purchases.

In contrast, some people believe Bitcoin's potential as a national currency is limited because Bitcoin's current framework is capable of making only seven transactions per second compared with Visa's credit card network which can handle a monolithic 65,000 transactions per second.

Note:
Some countries use Bitcoin to preserve value when national currencies are eroded by hyperinflation, as in Venezuela.

In addition, the issue of privacy is another affliction of Bitcoin because it provides sufficient privacy to give criminals cover while at the same time it's possible to trace transactions through a user's pseudonym. There is also the issue of Bitcoin's continual fluctuation of value, rising and falling in price with the inconsistencies seen in the ever-present surges and declines of the stock market.

A national currency needs more stability than Bitcoin presently appears capable of providing. However, what Bitcoin has provided, at least in the present day, is a window into the future that describes the potential of the blockchain technology upon which it is based, and the promise of an evolving awareness, application, and employment of an efficacious cryptocurrency.

It is generally agreed by many experts we are approaching the day when blockchain technology will be used as the underlying structure for centralized national currencies. It's clear that the form of money is moving from physical existence into digital representation, and blockchain technology has proven effective with securing this modern day transformation. Because blockchain technology can secure data and wealth and prevent hacking, it is likely to be the foundation upon which cryptocurrencies will be developed and provided.

Estonia was considering developing a national currency called the Estcoin in 2017, but was dissuaded by the European Central Bank. On the other hand, the United Kingdom's Bank of England received approval from King Charles in 2023 to proceed with the acceptance of cryptocurrencies, which would then influence other institutions to fall in line and accept the digital renaissance.

A national cryptocurrency is also regarded as a way to prevent illegal activity because even though anonymous ledgers are employed, police agencies can still track users and their financial information, making it difficult to conceal indiscretions.

Once the national banks and large corporations adopt blockchain technology and cryptocurrencies, smaller companies will need to follow the leaders and accept digital transactions for the exchange of wealth or secure information like medical and insurance records. Experts believe that in the next few years much of our daily exchanges will be seated on a blockchain foundation, possibly without our ever realizing it as corporations move forward with their planning and implementation.

Academic Studies

As blockchain and cryptocurrency interest increases, more and more academic studies are being conducted to understand various perspectives of value and application. In 2018, a university in South Korea and one in Finland combined their efforts to identify the extent of other academic research being conducted on blockchain technology related to the variety of topics, the challenges faced by the new industry, and potential future directions from a technical perspective.

Their research uncovered a total of 41 primary papers from scientific databases and the results showed that over 80% of the research conducted so far was focused on the Bitcoin system while less than 20% of the remaining academic research activities were focused on blockchain applications for such things as smart contracts and licensing.

Key:
Academic research is currently extremely limited, meaning this is an industry that needs a lot more study. This also suggests investors should be careful.

The majority of research centered on identifying blockchain limitations on privacy and security; proposed solutions were more academic than practical as they did not provide solutions based on concrete evidence, leading the two universities to conclude that academic research in this area was still in its infancy, with much more research needed as the technology evolves.

Academic interest has dramatically increased since 2013 when there were only two research papers, to 2015 when they was a total of 41 papers over a two-year period. The issue of scalability requires considerable thought, as does the issue of transaction speed.

Clearly, more research is needed on blockchain-based applications, and the value of emerging cryptocurrencies and their effect on national financial systems, adoption by the general public, prevention of use by criminal organizations, the application of smart contracts, the application of blockchain technology related to property licensing and domestic political voting, the possibility of an adoption of a global currency, and certainly dozens of other topics of profound interest for the 21st century's social and financial environment.

Notable Investors

The billionaire entrepreneur Mark Cuban is a strong supporter of blockchain technology. He has been quoted as saying the technology is "transformative", and is currently an advisor for a company called Radical App which will soon be releasing a blockchain messaging technology called Mercury Protocol. Mr. Cuban is also involved with Initial Coin Offerings, specifically token sales because "I think Blockchain is a great platform for future technology, future applications...just like the 'net and streaming created multiple great companies, I think blockchain will as well."

Cameron and Tyler Winklevoss, the American rowers and Internet entrepreneurs, were early promoters of Bitcoin and led a 2013 seed funding round for a Bitcoin trading startup called BitInstant. Since then, the twins have launched their own Bitcoin exchange called Gemini, and they have prospered well by being Bitcoin advocates; according to recent reports they are worth $1.3 billion in Bitcoin holdings.

The world-famous banker, Blythe Masters, a former executive at JP Morgan Chase, has stated that blockchain technology changes everything, and she is currently involved with designing software that will allow banks, investors, and other participants to use blockchain technology for trading loans, bonds, and a variety of other financial assets. "You should be taking this technology as seriously as you should have been taking the development of the Internet in the early 1990s. It's analogous to e-mail for money."[8]

Another advocate for blockchain technology and cryptocurrencies is the

Founders Fund, the Silicon Valley venture capital firm which is well regarded for its foresight with early investment in Facebook. One of its co-founders is the well-known investor and billionaire Peter Thiel, who is also one of the co-founders of PayPal. His counsel resulted in the purchase of over $15 million of Bitcoin for several of the investment funds at Founders Fund.

According to an interview with Fox Business Network anchor Maria Bartiromo, Thiel commented that people who are criticizing Bitcoin are "underestimating [it] especially because ... it's like a reserve form of money, it's like gold, and it's just a store of value. You don't need to use it to make payments. If Bitcoin ends up being the cyber equivalent of gold it has a great potential left."

---

[8] Bloomburg, August 31, 2015. Edward Robinson and Matthew Leising, www.bloomburg.com

Examples of Companies Using and Investing in Blockchain Technology

Corporate interest in blockchain technology is commanding the attention of industry leaders and investors as nearly $250,000,000 in venture capital money was raised in the first half of 2017. Curiously, banks are presently the biggest proponents of blockchain technology. This may be because banking executives foresee that blockchain technology will improve their efficiency with clearing and settlement, resulting in savings that could total $10 billion or more. With a ratio in savings to cost of 40:1, bank leadership is enthusiastic about the possibilities.

Banking institutions have been seeking a solution for shared digital utility for recording their customers' identities and maintaining them with regular updates, which is mandated by anti-money laundering laws. Blockchain's cryptographic protection and its capacity for sharing regularly updated records with many participants appears to be the answer they have been seeking.

Key:
Some corporations are creating their own corporate cryptocurrency, suggesting that cryptocurrency is being established as a standard means for doing business. Current companies: Facebook in cooperation with Libra; JPMorgan Chase (JPMCoin), Walmart, and in progress are Mitsubishi, Amazon, and Google.

One of the earliest retailers to embrace the blockchain platform and accept cryptocurrency was Overstock.com, whose shares jumped up 265% in 2017. In December 2017, the company made history by being the first publicly traded company to issue its stock through an ICO, distributing more than 126,000 company shares in this manner.

Another important corporate participant is chipmaker NVIDIA, the American technology company located in Santa Clara, California. The corporation's intention appears to be a strategy for providing NVIDIA chips for blockchain technology; as more people get involved with mining cryptocurrencies, the sale of NVIDIA products will expand. NVIDIA's rival, AMD (Advanced Micro Devices), is also becoming heavily involved with positioning itself to take advantage of anticipated growth in the use of blockchain technology and cryptocurrency mining.

The latest news is that Walmart and British Airways are looking into blockchain technology's ability to improve complex global supply chains. In addition, Microsoft has about 40 blockchain patents filed; Fidelity Investments has around 14 patents filed; technology giant QUALCOMM has 20 blockchain patents filed; and there is keen interest and activity from Bank of America, Red Hat, Dell, MasterCard, Google, Cisco, Hewlett-Packard, Huawei, Fujitsu, and others.

As these corporate giants move into developing blockchain technology for their particular niche services, it's likely to be a short wait before blockchain technology becomes the new standard of operation.

Summary

Clearly, our communal future will be based on blockchain technology for services of all kinds and in all industries, and become the likely standard for the secure transaction of cryptocurrencies. It's interesting to reflect that we are on the cusp of an entirely new technology whose horizons are beyond our capacity to see and fully appreciate.

Just as when Columbus landed in the West Indies, his ability to foresee the rocky coast of the Pacific shoreline in Northern California and all the incredible geographic landmarks and material opportunities that lay in front of his sandy footprint was even less myopic than our current inability to fully envision how blockchain technology will transform the economic landscape of our digitally interactive systems and subsequent norm of human social behavior for the rest of the 21st century...yes, and beyond.

Chapter 13: Review Questions

1. Blockchain technology and the development of cryptocurrencies is similar to the tulipmania of the 17th century. True or false?

   A. True

   B. False

2. Which of the following statements is false?

   A. Some cryptocurrencies will not survive the test of time

   B. Some countries are using bitcoins as a medium of exchange because the fiat currency is hyperinflated

   C. Bitcoin's present downside is that it cannot process transactions very quickly

   D. None of these statements is false

   E. A and C are true

   F. A and B are true

3. How many transactions per second can Bitcoin complete?

   A. 5

   B. 7

   C. 1,263

   D. 65,000

4. One of the reasons bitcoin may not become a national cryptocurrency is because its value fluctuates too much. True or false?

A. True

B. False

5. Another downside to Bitcoin is that it provides sufficient privacy to hide criminal activity. True or false?

A. True

B. False

6. Which country was going to have the world's first national cryptocurrency, but was dissuaded by the European Central Bank?

A. Latvia

B. Estonia

C. Lithuania

D. Baklava

7. Academic studies on block chain technology and crypto currencies is prolific. True or false?

A. True

B. False

Chapter 13: Answers

1. Blockchain technology and the development of cryptocurrencies is similar to the tulipmania of the 17th century. True or false?

A. True

B. False

Answer: B. False. The "tulip mania" was an entirely speculative event. While investors need to be careful about investing in block chain technology and crypto currencies, the reason for hesitancy is because this is new technology and a new form of digital currency, both of which will need time to become established means of economic practice. Both have inherent value, unlike the Dutch tulips which were initially thought to be rare but were found to be common.

2. Which of the following statements is false?

A. Some cryptocurrencies will not survive the test of time

B. Some countries are using bitcoins as a medium of exchange because the fiat currency is hyperinflated

C. Bitcoin's present downside is that it cannot process transactions very quickly

D. None of these statements is false

E. A and C are true

F. A and B are true

Answer: D. All of the statements are true. Investors should be cautious because some cryptocurrencies have already failed; the cryptocurrency industry is so new that only very few cryptocurrencies have the beginning of a reliable track record. Also, both Venezuela and Zimbabwe are using Bitcoins as a more reliable form of economic exchange than their own national currency because of hyperinflation. Lastly, bit coin transactions are currently processed at the speed of seven per second; this may limit bit coin's ability to be a standard of currency and may instead force upon it the role of an investment asset.

3. How many transactions per second can Bitcoin complete?

A. 5

B. 7

C. 1,263

D. 65,000

Answer: B. Presently, Bitcoin can only process seven transactions per second. This may limit Bitcoin's potential to become a currency and may consign Bitcoin to being an investment asset. By comparison, Visa's credit card network can handle 65,000 transactions per second.

4. One of the reasons bitcoin may not become a national cryptocurrency is because its value fluctuates too much. True or false?

A. True

B. False

Answer: A. True. A national currency needs to be stable so citizens can rely on its steady value. Bitcoin's value fluctuates too much at the present time for it to be a wholesome candidate. This may be true for all cryptocurrencies that are not established by government.

5. Another downside to Bitcoin is that it provides sufficient privacy to hide criminal activity. True or false?

A. True

B. False

Answer: A. True. Governments are concerned that Bitcoin may be a source of funding for criminal and terrorist activities.

6. Which country was going to have the world's first national cryptocurrency, but was dissuaded by the European Central Bank?

A. Latvia

B. Estonia

C. Lithuania

D. Baklava

Answer: B. In 2017, the government of Estonia was developing the Estcoin, and was on track for being the world's first national cryptocurrency when the European Central Bank admonished them. Not wanting to jeopardize their European Union status, Estonia deferred to the pressure. However, in 2023, the EU adopted new rules on cryptoassets. Estonia was a pioneer and suffered because of it.

7. Academic studies on block chain technology and crypto currencies is prolific. True or false?

A. True

B. False

Answer: B. False. There is a lack of academic study at this time. Advancing knowledge about the applications of blockchain technology and the employment of cryptocurrencies would be welcome and could bring fame and fortune.

Glossary

This glossary contains popular words associated with cryptocurrencies, investment, and portfolio management.

Please note that the definitions provided are simplified for general understanding, and the actual usage and technical nuances of these terms may vary in specific contexts within the cryptocurrency industry, investments, and portfolio management.

Air drops: Air drops are when free tokens or coins are distributed to the users or owners of a blockchain or cryptocoin.

Altcoin: An altcoin is any alternative cryptocurrency that appeared after Bitcoin was established as a reliably tradeable currency.

Bitcoin: A unit of cryptocurrency. Also the protocol used to create the first decentralized currency.

Bitgold: Regarded as the predecessor of bitcoin, this currency existed only academically.

Block: A unit of data that contains a unique cash, and the hash of the preceding block.

Blockchain: A continuously updated record of data that secures proven information by consensus, removing the need for validation by third-party intermediaries.

b-money: An early digital currency developed by Wei Dai as "an anonymous, distributed electronic cash system".

CBDC: Central Bank Digital Currency. This is a digital version of a country's currency that is issued by its central bank. CBDCs are designed to be used in everyday transactions, similar to cash.

Central control: In the cryptocurrency ecosystem, central control refers to the presence of a single authority or entity that governs, manages, or oversees the operation, transactions, and decisions of a monetary network, as opposed to decentralized systems where control is distributed among participants.

Chicago Mercantile Exchange (CME): The CME, or CME Group, facilitates the trading of futures, options, cash and OTC markets.

Cold storage: Storing cryptocurrency in a device that is completely off-line, like a hardware wallet. This is the most secure form of storage for owners of cryptocurrency who want to store their wealth over the long-term.

Consensus: One of the three elements that secures a block from fraud by requiring at least 51% of a blockchain network to agree the block is authentic.

Cryptocurrency: A form of currency that is protected from fraud with cryptography.

Cryptography: Algorithms written to prevent easy access and safeguard important information.

Cyber Unit: An SEC criminal investigation unit that targets cyber-related misconduct and threats.

Cypherpunk: A person advocating for the widespread use of privacy-enhancing technologies and cryptography to create systemic social and political change.

dApp development: A dApp is a computer code used on a decentralized peer-to- peer network, as opposed to running on centralized servers.

dApps: Decentralized applications; these are applications that can be used by digital technology, providing services or information from a decentralized source on a blockchain. You can use a dApp to buy and sell cryptocurrency, for example.

Decentralized: This term means that an activity is controlled by several organizations or systems, rather than a single one.

DeFi: Decentralized finance. Decentralized finance (DeFi) is a peer-to-peer financial system that uses blockchain technology to provide banking and financial services. DeFi aims to reduce costs and transaction times by removing traditional financial middlemen like banks.

Desktop wallet: A desktop wallet is the most common type of digital currency wallet, usually consisting of an application located on a user's computer screen.

Digital: Signals or data represented by a series of 0 or 1, or both.

Digital currency: A form of electronic currency.

Discount: A monetary value that decreases the price of the property to attract a buyer.

Distributed ledger: A database that is shared and synchronized across multiple nodes in a network, such as computers or organizations. Distributed ledgers allow participants to record, verify, and execute transactions without a central authority, such as a bank or auditor.

Distributed transparent ledger: A collection of data distributed to every node in a network.

Double coincidence of wants: The simultaneous intention of a seller to sell and a buyer to buy a good or service.

Double spend problem: A concern that digital currency be used more than once; this was resolved with a cryptographic hashing algorithm developed by the NSA.

ERC-20 tokens: ERC are the initials for Ethereum Request for Comments which is the process used for recommending improvements to the Ethereum network. The number 20 was the proposal identification number for authorizing tokens on the Ethereum network. The tokens are an asset that can be authorized for various uses on the Ethereum network.

Estcoin: A national currency that was being developed by Estonia. This could have been the world's first national cryptocurrency. Alas, it was not to be. Instead, the Commonwealth of Dominica in the Caribbean was the first in 2022.

ETF: An Exchange Traded Fund is an investment fund traded on stock exchanges.

Ethereum (ETC): An alternative blockchain network that can be used for its cryptocurrency called Ether, and for other blockchain purposes. The Ethereum blockchain is more versatile than the Bitcoin blockchain.

Exchange: An online exchange is a company that offers cryptocurrency for purchase, trade, or sale.

Feerate: The fee offered by the initiator of a transaction to miners for processing and confirming the transaction.

Fiat: Formal authorization by a government or group.

Fintech: Technology that supports banking and financial services.

Fungible: Capable of being duplicated, mutually interchangeable.

Gas Fees: The compensation paid to miners and stakers for making transactions possible on the blockchains.

Hardware wallet: This level of wallet is dedicated hardware built specifically to contain cryptocurrency and hold it securely. A hardware wallet can access online transactions to retrieve data and can then go off-line and be transported for convenience and security.

Hash: The unique set of sequenced numbers and letters used to identify only one specific block of data.

Hashcash: A proof-of-work system created by Adam Back to protect information from manipulation and fraud, originally developed as a means for controlling spam.

Hashrate: The speed at which a hash is calculated. A high hashrate increases a miner's chances of being paid a transaction fee for processing a transaction and creating a new block.

Hot storage: Storing cryptocurrency in a device that's directly connected to the Internet, and easy to access funds.

Initial Coin Offering: An ICO is used by founders of a cryptocurrency to raise funds to capitalize a company and develop essential components needed to secure the company's presence in the marketplace.

Initial Real Estate Offering (IREO): The initial proposal of a real estate property available for purchase to attract investors participating in a blockchain real estate network using cryptocurrency.

Investment Policy Statement (IPS): A formal set of rules an investor follows for buying, holding, and selling investments to build wealth and remove the emotions of fear and greed from the trading process.

Liquid real estate: Real estate value that can be easily purchased or sold through a blockchain using cryptotokens as the medium of exchange.

Liquidity: The characteristic of being easily exchanged between one form and another.

Meme: An image, video, piece of text, etc., typically humorous, which can spread rapidly on the Internet.

Meme coins: These are a cryptocurrency derived from an Internet meme, usually a cultural or humorous derivation such as Shiba Inu or Pepe.

Metaverse: A virtual-reality space where users can interact with a computer-generated environment and other users as well.

Miner: A person who uses computers to calculate algorithms for mining bitcoins and other transactions, and is rewarded with transaction fees in the form of digital currency.

Mining: The process of calculating algorithmic problems for transaction fees in the form of digital currency.

Mobile wallet: A mobile wallet is a wallet connected through an app on a smart phone.

Monero: A cryptocurrency privacy coin that offers a deeper level of privacy.

Mt. Gox: In 2014 this Bitcoin exchange in Tokyo, Japan participated in over 70% of all Bitcoin transactions worldwide, and went bankrupt after losing approximately $450 million through theft.

NFT: Nonfungible token. An NFT is a unique (one of a kind) digital asset representing the ownership of a digital or physical item. NFTs are stored on a blockchain.

Node: A member of a blockchain network.

Nonce: A nonce is a 32-bit field composed of random numbers that can be used only once, and set so the block's hash will contain a sequence of leading zeros.

Nonfungible: Unique; unable to be duplicated.

Online wallet: An online wallet is web-based. An app is not downloaded to a user's computer, but instead the user accesses the wallet through a website's server.

Open source: Software code that is publicly posted on the Internet, allowing anyone to be able to copy, paste, find bugs and submit updates to the source code.

Paper wallet: Used to avoid keeping digital data about a user's currency online, a paper wallet requires printing a QR code for the public and private keys, allowing the user to send and receive digital currency without having to store currency information online.

Privacy coins: Privacy coins use a disseminated public ledger but employ a different technology that camouflages transactions. The amount of the transaction is not disguised, but the trail from sender to recipient is not revealed.

Private key: A private key is a secret, alphanumeric password/number used to spend/send bitcoins between Bitcoin addresses. It acts as the user's digital signature.

Proof of Importance: One of the three proofs that secures a block's authenticity, the proof of importance is an algorithm that determines which miner is most authorized to verify a transaction by assigning a degree of importance to the miner. The degree of importance is established by several factors, such as the length of time a miner has been part of the network, or how often other miners have accepted information generated by the miner as a measure of credibility.

Proof of Stake: One of the three proofs that secures a block's authenticity, the proof of stake states that a degree of authority is assigned to how many bitcoins a miner owns, inferring that the more stake a miner has, the more likely they are to be careful about analyzing transactions which could affect their own holdings.

Proof of work: One of the three elements that secures a block from fraud by requiring a solution to a complex algorithm.

Proof-of-Stake (PoS): A cryptocurrency consensus mechanism for processing data such as transactions.

Public address: The public address is an alphanumeric address/number derived from private keys by using cryptographic math functions, and is used to publicly receive bitcoins. A Bitcoin public address always starts with the number 1.

Public key: A public key is the public alphanumeric password/number used to spend/send bitcoins between Bitcoin addresses.

Q coins; QQ coins: An early form of digital currency popular in China.

Satoshi Nakamoto: An unknown individual or group of people who solved the double spend problem and allowed bitcoin to be used as the first secure digital currency.

Scrypt: The name of the proof-of-work algorithm used by Litecoin, which makes mining coins easier and cheaper than mining Bitcoins.

SEC (U.S. Securities and Exchange Commission): The SEC is an independent agency of the U.S. government that enforces federal securities laws.

Seed phrase: A seed phrase is a list of words that serves as a backup to recover cryptocurrency funds.

Server farm: A server farm is a facility dedicated to housing hundreds of servers that process and store digital information.

SHA-256: The name of Bitcoin's proof-of-work algorithm.

Silk Road: The Silk Road was a black market using bitcoin currency, and was eventually terminated by U.S. law enforcement with its founder sentenced to double life + 40 years in prison. Ross Ulbricht has since received a full and complete pardon by President Donald Trump.

Smart contract: A self-executing program stored on a blockchain that automatically enforces, verifies, or executes the terms of an agreement when predefined conditions are met. It eliminates the need for intermediaries, ensuring transparency, security, and efficiency in transactions.

Sponsor: A person who acts as an agent for the presentation or sale of an object.

Spot price: The current price of an item in the market.

Two-Factor Authentication (2FA): A system that uses two authentication steps to verify data.

User: A participant on a decentralized network who sends and receives payments from other users and pays a small fee to the miners for verifying transactions.

Wallet: A cryptocurrency wallet contains the user's private and public keys, allowing the user to send and receive cryptocoins, and acts as a personal ledger, keeping track of all transactions. There are currently five types of cryptocurrency wallets: desktop wallet, online wallet, mobile wallet, hardware wallet, and paper wallet.

Wallet Import Format (WIF): The WIF is the process for encoding a private key to make it easier to transmit on a blockchain.

Web3 or Web 3.0: Web3 is the next generation of the Internet, providing users with more control over their data and identities. It's also known as Web 3.0, the decentralized web.

Zcash: A privacy coin that uses a public blockchain and offers users the opportunity to conceal the sender, recipient, and amount of the transaction, or choose the option to be transparent. The level of privacy is sufficient for most people and as it turns out, presently only a small number of its users choose the privacy features.

About the Author

Joe Maas

CFA, CFP®, CLU®, ChFC,
MSFS, CCIM™, CVA, ABAR, CM&AA

Meet Joe Maas, an esteemed financial professional with an illustrious career spanning over three decades. As the Chief Investment Officer and lead portfolio manager at Synergy Asset Management LLC (SAM), Joe is dedicated to providing comprehensive investment management services to a diverse clientele comprising individual investors, business owners, and financial advisors.

Joe's expertise is anchored in a multifaceted approach that combines deep fundamental and economic analysis, in-depth industry research, consultations with his network of industry experts, and a keen application of quantitative methods and technical analysis.

Within his role, Joe doesn't limit himself to the analysis of existing investments; he also dedicates himself to assessing prospective opportunities, all with the aim of preserving his position as an industry thought leader and staying at the forefront of the investment industry's evolution.

Behind Joe's extensive knowledge of the financial industry is an unrelenting drive to continuously expand his understanding of investment management. This quest for excellence has led him to achieve certification from distinguished organizations and attain a host of globally recognized professional designations.

Among these achievements, Joe proudly holds the prestigious Chartered Financial Analyst (CFA) Charterholder designation, a testament to his mastery in the investment profession.

In addition to a CFA Charterholder, Joe is a Certified Financial Planner™ (CFP®) and Chartered Financial Consultant (ChFC), equipped to offer comprehensive advanced financial planning services. His diverse skill set extends to life insurance and estate planning as a chartered life underwriter (CLU®).

He also excels as a certified commercial investment member (CCIMTM), demonstrating his prowess in the realm of commercial and investment real estate. In 2000, Joe earned his Master of Science in Financial Services (MSFS) from The American College, further solidifying his expertise in the field.

Beyond his proficiency in investment and financial planning, Joe brings a wealth of expertise and hands-on experience tailored to the distinct requirements of business owners. Joe holds the coveted title of Certified Valuation Analyst (CVA) and boasts accreditation in business appraisal review (ABAR).

Furthermore, he brings to the table his expertise as a Certified Merger and Acquisition Advisor (CM&AA), a skill set honed in the intricate world of purchasing and divesting middle-market companies, with revenues spanning from $5 million to $500 million.

Joe Maas is more than just a financial expert; he is a visionary leader deeply devoted to assisting clients in navigating the complexities of the financial world, aiming to help them achieve their financial goals to the best of his abilities.

Contributing Author

Eryka Gemma

Eryka Gemma is a published author and professional speaker on digital assets and the decentralized ecosystem.

From a young age, Eryka had a passion for aviation, flying her first airplane at the age of 16. Her professional career started in finance in the aircraft trading and leasing division. Eryka's affinity for technology allowed her to become a consultant implementing technology systems. The switch to blockchain occurred when she started to explore security tokens and their potential effects on traditional markets.

Due to her grassroots nature, she is known in the Miami tech scene as a catalyst of Miami's evolution as the crypto capital of the Americas. In 2018, Eryka opened the Blockchain Center in Miami, a physical location that served the city as an incubation hub fostering education in South Florida.

Eryka is an investor and consultant in the digital asset ecosystem, bringing value through public relations, strategy, and a deep understanding of the technology.

Made in the USA
Columbia, SC
30 June 2025